4/95

Running Dog, Paper Tiger

by
Simon Johnston

Playwrights Canada Press
Toronto • Canada

Running Dog, Paper Tiger © Simon Johnston, 1995

Playwrights Canada Press is the publishing imprint of:
Playwrights Union of Canada
54 Wolseley Street, 2nd floor, Toronto, Ontario, M5T 1A5
Tel (416) 703-0201; Fax (416) 703-0059
E-mail: cdplays@interlog.com; Internet: www.puc.ca

Playwrights Canada Press operates with the generous assistance of The Canada Council for the Arts—Writing and Publishing Section, and the Ontario Arts Council, Literature Office.

Canadian Cataloguing in Publication Data

Johnston, Simon
    Running dog, paper tiger

A play.
ISBN 0-88754-556-4

I. Title

PS8569.O39174R86 1998   C812'.54   C98-930298-9
PR9199.3.J65R86   1998

First edition: May 1998
Printed and bound: Hignell Printing Ltd, Manitoba, Canada

Simon Johnston was born and raised in Hong Kong, and emigrated to Canada thirty years ago. He has worked in Canadian theatre for over twenty years as a playwright and director. Other plays include *Tales of the Arabian Nights* (1997), *A Nightingale Sang* (1998), and *The Steamer Atlantic* (1998). He has also written six radio plays for CBC Drama and Morningside; drama for CBC Television; the novel *Lion Dance*; and a children's book entitled *A Song for Harmonica*. Simon was Artistic Director of the Lighthouse Festival from 1987 to 1994, and previous to that was Artistic Director at Press Theatre, Resident Director at the Banff Centre, and Staff Director at Toronto Arts Productions (Canadian Stage). He has directed in numerous theatres across Canada, and has taught theatre and drama at colleges and universities. He currently lives in London, Ontario.

Author's Introduction

This is a play about loyalty and identity. I started writing it in 1994 as a reaction to the intense debate over the consequences of the Quebec referendum. Who would I be loyal to if my country was split apart, what would I ultimately become and what choice did I have in answering these questions? To paraphrase Robertson Davies, "I am living in a country which is constantly in a state of becoming and never is."

I find it interesting that as a writer pondering these issues, what came out was a story about a mixed-race family living in Hong Kong in 1967 that was pushed to face these questions as a result of political influences beyond its control. The characters in this play are forced to make decisions about who they are, what they are loyal to, and how they ultimately will live with their decisions.

When the next referendum comes, will it be regarded as just another annoyance, or will it be embraced as an opportunity to reassess the process of becoming? The choice is ours. Carpe diem!

I wish to thank the following for their assistance during the development of this play: Arthur Milner, former Artistic Director of The Great Canadian Theatre Company (Ottawa) for the original commission; Theatre BC for selecting it as Winner of the 1995 National Playwrighting Award; and Marion DeVries and Jocelyn Hublau of Cahoots Theatre (Toronto) for including it in their 1996 "Lift Off" series of workshops.

I reserve special thanks for Rebecca Cann, who was my script editor and dramaturge. And, of course, for Sheila, who remains my artistic conscience.

Production History

Running Dog, Paper Tiger was commissioned by the Great Canadian Theatre Company in 1994-95. It was selected Winner of Theatre BC's National Playwrighting Competition in 1995, and was included in the Cahoots Theatre Projects "Lift Off" workshop series.

The world premiere production of *Running Dog, Paper Tiger* was performed at the Gateway Theatre in Richmond, BC on October 16, 1997, with the following cast and crew:

MARK SIMMONS	Haig Sutherland
MATTHEW SIMMONS	Ian Leung
CAMPBELL WONG	John James Hong
GEORGE SIMMONS	Paul Batten
HELEN SIMMONS	Marilyn Norry
SARAH WOTFORD	Tiffany Lyndall-Knight
CHIEF INSPECTOR STERLING	Eric Gordon

Producer: Ken Neufeld
Director: Bill Dow
Assistant Director: John Keith
Set and Costumes Designer: Marti Wright
Lighting Designer: Adrian Muir
Sound Designer: John Mills-Cockell
Stage Manager: Mary Kavanagh
Assistant Stage Manager: Lorraine Hamilton

The Characters

MARK SIMMONS
Mixed race. Appears as a fifteen and thirty-five year old.

MATTHEW SIMMONS
Mixed race. Appears as a seventeen and thirty-seven year old.

CAMPBELL WONG
Chinese houseboy and friend to Mark and Matthew.
Appears as a sixteen and thirty-six year old.

GEORGE SIMMONS
Mixed race. Father of Mark and Matthew.

HELEN SIMMONS
Mixed race. George's wife.

SARAH WOTFORD
British. Mark's girlfriend. Appears as a fifteen and thirty-five year old.

CHIEF SUPERINTENDENT STERLING
British. Chief Superintendent of the Hong Kong Special Branch.

Production Notes

"Running Dog" is a literal translation of the Cantonese expression used to describe a cowardly person. "Paper Tiger" describes one who appears dangerous but is actually as insubstantial as paper.

The text provides phonetic approximations of the Cantonese spoken in the play. For performance purposes, accuracy in this dialect would, of course, be invaluable. English translation of the Cantonese dialogue is provided in square brackets.

Members of the Simmons family are of mixed race and should not look Chinese. The actor playing Matthew Simmons may double as Chief Inspector Sterling.

Act One

Hong Kong, 1987.

MARK *and* SARAH SIMMONS *are
kneeling in prayer, in the chapel of a
Catholic hospital. Suddenly, we hear a
scream offstage, followed by voices.
Someone is trying to get into the chapel
but is being prevented from doing so.*
SARAH *reacts, but* MARK *remains
poised. The voices get closer until,
finally,* CAMPBELL WONG *bursts
through the door.*

CAMPBELL   Where is she?

SARAH   Campbell!

CAMPBELL   Where is she?

SARAH *looks at the two men, then exits.*

CAMPBELL   I'm waiting.

No response.

Well?

No response.

CAMPBELL   Goddammit, Mark! You owe me that much!

MARK   Owe you?

CAMPBELL   Yes. I came here in good faith, but you left
instructions preventing me from seeing her. I
telephoned you—eight times! You never answered
me. Now she's dead. I have a right—

MARK   A right? Hong Kong is still British territory and here you have no rights—

CAMPBELL   What the hell are you talking about? This is not about—

MARK   Can't wait to throw your weight around—

CAMPBELL   This is not about—

MARK   Well, you people will have to wait—

CAMPBELL   "You people"...? Look, which funeral home is it?

MARK   Find out, I'm sure you can.

CAMPBELL   You are being childish and petulant.

MARK does not respond.

It was Helen's wish to see me before she died.... Here, read this.... Sarah wrote me... it says she wants me to honour her remains and... well, here, you can see for yourself.... It was her wish—yes, mine also. I'm here to fulfill the Chinese traditions— I'm here—

MARK   You are *not* a member of this family.

CAMPBELL   I have *always* been a member of this family—

MARK   No—

CAMPBELL   I have a right!

MARK   After what you did to my family, you have no rights!

Pause.

CAMPBELL   You must... we both must... put that horrible moment to rest.

MARK turns away.

CAMPBELL	Listen to me— I know you still hear their screams arcing across twenty years— You have to understand—
MARK	No—
CAMPBELL	I, too, can still hear his voice. That—
GEORGE	(*off*) Damn!

> CAMPBELL *and* MARK *stare at each other for a moment. They both look in the direction from which the voice came.*
>
> *Then the lights change, and we are in 1967 Hong Kong, in the apartment home of the* SIMMONS *family.* GEORGE SIMMONS *enters, holding two passports.* MARK *and* CAMPBELL *watch from "1987."*

GEORGE	Helen!

> HELEN SIMMONS *enters. She is holding a camera with a flash attachment.*

GEORGE	Is there film in that thing?
HELEN	Yes, dear, just loaded it.
GEORGE	Good—
HELEN	What's all this about?
GEORGE	Have a look at those.
HELEN	Passports.
GEORGE	Look at this page... huh? And here, on this one too... read it, go on....
HELEN	Expires 1968. We have a year to go—
GEORGE	No—this, this.

> MATTHEW SIMMONS *appears "above."*
> HELEN *examines the indicated page on*
> *one of the passports, then looks at the*
> *same page on the second passport.*

GEORGE   Huh, y'see. It's stroked out: "Holder has the right
of abode in the United Kingdom." Stroked out, do
y'see? Huh.

> MATTHEW *whistles a signal.* MARK
> *and* CAMPBELL *look "up" and*
> *instinctively whistle a response, then exit.*

HELEN   I never noticed.... We are not welcome in
England....

GEORGE   Where are my medals?

> *He doesn't wait for a response, and exits*
> *to fetch them.*

HELEN   We have to stay no matter what happens.

> MARK *and* CAMPBELL *enter "above" on*
> *the roof to join* MATTHEW. *They are all*
> *teenagers, dressed as schoolboys.* HELEN
> *winds the film forward, puts in a*
> *flashbulb, etc.*

MATTHEW   Have you got it?

> CAMPBELL *unwraps his handkerchief,*
> *which holds a "Double Banger."*

MARK   Wow!

MATTHEW   *Leung for bow!* [Double Banger!]

MARK   How much?

CAMPBELL   A street hawker dropped it during a police raid.
Ng-gor geep jor kui lah! [I picked it up.]

MARK   *Bay ng-aw tie-ah.* [Let me have a look.]

MATTHEW	Got any matches?
CAMPBELL	Here.
MARK	The police have banned these—
MATTHEW	Nah, look, the powder has leaked out the side, it'll only go "phut."

> MATTHEW *raises the firecracker up like a sword.* MARK *and* CAMPBELL *place their right hands on* MATTHEW*'s.*

MATTHEW	All for one!
ALL	And one for all!

> MATTHEW *unfurls a long fuse attached to the firecracker.* CAMPBELL *lights the fuse, and the boys back away.* GEORGE *enters, holding a bar of WWII medals.* HELEN *helps him pin them on.*

GEORGE	Four generations we have been here! Four!
HELEN	Yes, Eurasians built this country.
GEORGE	Don't! Don't use that word! We are English!

> *GEORGE takes the medals from HELEN.*

I'll do it, I'll do it. You focus that thing. Where shall I stand?

HELEN	There.
GEORGE	My people came here from Dunfree in the 1870s, and that entitles us to pass as English. *(he poses)* How's this? And another thing, we fought in the last war, for King and Country. Everyone—the Poles, the Czechs—got either British or American passports after the war. Why is there one set of rules for those people and a different set for us?

GEORGE   With these damned Red Guard demonstrations all over the bloody place, we need that document. Ow! Damn, pricked myself.

HELEN   Hair....

>   GEORGE *smooths his hair.*

Shirt....

>   GEORGE *straightens his shirt.*

Will the demonstrations lead to violence?

GEORGE   We're on twenty-four-hour alert, as of today. People are not saying it, but you know as well as I that they are packing....

HELEN   Just in case....

GEORGE   Better?

HELEN   The light's behind you, stand here.

GEORGE   Arthur is organizing a petition to the Colonial Office, with photos of vets. We deserve protection. But without proper passports— We'll need money, cash. How about here?

HELEN   Yes.

GEORGE   Right, can you get a head-and-shoulder shot?

HELEN   Hold still.

GEORGE   The Reds will make their move in the spring, not now. Damn commies ran over Shanghai in '49, just like that.... I lost everything.... Now they want Hong Kong. Well, it won't be so easy this time.

>   HELEN *takes a photo. The flash goes off and the rocket explodes with an enormous bang, simultaneously.*

GEORGE	What the hell!

HELEN, MATTHEW, MARK, and CAMPBELL all yell out simultaneously:

HELEN	Oh, my God!
MATTHEW	Holy!
MARK	Wow!
CAMPBELL	Wa-hi!
GEORGE	Goddammit! What the hell was that? Who's up there!

The boys freeze.

Boy! Who's up there? Matthew?

MATTHEW	What's he doing home so early?
GEORGE	Do I have to come up and see for myself?
MATTHEW	No.
GEORGE	Matthew? What did I say about fireworks? Is Mark there too?

Pause.

MATTHEW	No....
GEORGE	Anyone else?

MATTHEW signals the other two to leave. CAMPBELL and MARK exit.

MATTHEW	No....
GEORGE	Get down here. NOW!

MATTHEW exits to go "downstairs."

GEORGE   What the hell is the matter with him? He's slacking off at school, slacking off at cricket. How will he hope to ever get into a good law school—

HELEN   George—

GEORGE   Stop protecting him. You are just like your mother, you always want to cover everything up—

> MATTHEW *enters.* HELEN *plays with the wedding ring on her finger.*

That was a Double Banger.

MATTHEW   Yes.

GEORGE   How will it look if my son was arrested for possession of illegal fireworks? Where's Mark?

MATTHEW   I don't know.

GEORGE   Mark!

MATTHEW   I didn't think it would make such a bang.

GEORGE   I told you boys, only small crackers. Didn't I?

MATTHEW   Yes.

> MARK *and* CAMPBELL *enter.*

HELEN   Mark, wash your hands.

GEORGE   Show me those hands first.

> MARK *shows his hands, reluctantly.*

HELEN   Campbell, help me with the tea.

> CAMPBELL *exits.* GEORGE *inspects* MARK'*s fingers. He smells the gunpowder.*

GEORGE   You were with him.

MATTHEW	I was alone.
GEORGE	Liar!

> GEORGE *slaps* MATTHEW *hard across the face.* MATTHEW *crumbles to the floor.* GEORGE *turns to* MARK *and raises his hand to strike.* HELEN *stands.*

HELEN	Stop it!
GEORGE	Liars, all of you. And another thing. I don't want you hanging around with Campbell. He's the houseboy, and he could be a commie—
MATTHEW	He's not a commie.
GEORGE	Whazat?
MATTHEW	Campbell is not a commie!

> GEORGE *looks at* HELEN.

GEORGE	For that you can go without your tea and dinner. Get out of my sight. Both of you.

> MATTHEW *and* MARK *exit.*

Boy!

HELEN	Matthew said he was alone.
GEORGE	Oh, they were all three together on this, alright.

> CAMPBELL *enters.*

I suppose you had nothing to do with it? Huh? Don't bother answering, I've had enough of lying. Fetch me my tea. Come back here. Don't you look at me like that. If I find out that you brought illegal fireworks into my home, you'll be out on your arse—savvy?

CAMPBELL	Yes.

GEORGE	"Yes" what.
CAMPBELL	Yes, sir.
GEORGE	That's better. I take you in, send you to school with my sons, and this is how you repay me. Now, give these a buff, will you? Well?

> *Pause.*

CAMPBELL	The tea....
HELEN	I'll get it.

> HELEN *exits to the kitchen.* GEORGE *sits. He stretches one leg out, presenting his boot to be shined, and takes up a newspaper.* CAMPBELL *spits on* GEORGE*'s boot.*
>
> MATTHEW *enters on the roof. He is in a titanic struggle to hold back tears. After a moment,* MARK *enters. He is holding binoculars, a notebook, and the local "Shipping News."* MATTHEW *turns away from* MARK.

MARK	It's almost even' tide. .. There... yes, here she comes, just steamin' along... want to see...?

> *MARK makes a note in his notebook.*

	Li-y-moon Pass, right on time, just before the sunset tide.... It's sitting very low... I can't see the Plimsoll Line... that's illegal isn't it...? No, it's not at the centre.... Do they ever put it on the starboard side...? Does it hurt?
MATTHEW	The Plimsoll line must be below the water....
MARK	Wow, then its overloaded.... They'll get a fine, won't they...? What are they carrying... let's see... *(checking the "Shipping News")* The *Inca Maru, Inca Maru*....

MATTHEW	*Inca Maru*... twelve thousand tons... fruits.
MARK	Um....
MATTHEW	Mangos from Manila?
MARK	Bananas from Bombay?
MATTHEW	East, not west.
MARK	Um....
MATTHEW	Pears from Panama, apples from Appalachia....
MARK	Bananas from Brazil!
MATTHEW	There are no bananas in Brazil, only nuts— Ow!
MARK	What?
MATTHEW	Nothing. I bit my tongue when....

MATTHEW *takes the binoculars.*

MARK	Does it hurt?
MATTHEW	Hurt. I'll tell you about pain someday.... There's the last one for tonight: *SS Rotterdam*, leaving early, filled with tourists, here to see the Chinese New Year, disappointed because there are no fireworks to liven up their evenings.
MARK	Must be dinner-time for them.
MATTHEW	Cocktail sausages, little ham and cheese thingies, sardines on toast, shrimp with dip....
MARK	Mmmmm
MATTHEW	Caviar....
BOTH	Eeew, don't want that!
MARK	Entrées!

MATTHEW	Roast beef with mashed potatoes....
MARK	Baked, I like them baked....
MATTHEW	Baked for him, mashed for me....
MARK	With sour cream, lots of sour cream....
MATTHEW	No vegetables, thank you.
MARK	Fried noodles....
MATTHEW	With green onions and lovely bits of pork....
MARK	Cooked with ginger, soy sauce, and sesame seeds....
MATTHEW	Steaming crab legs, crack-crack, slide the meat out, dip it in a sweet-and-sour sauce, put it in your mouth and let it sit there— Ow, damn!
MARK	What?
MATTHEW	Damn, damn, bit my tongue again. I think it's swollen. They'll regret this. The next time I'm going to—

> GEORGE *rises, looks at his reflection on the toecaps of his boots.*

GEORGE	Huh. I'll make a houseboy out of you yet. Helen! I'm off. No time for the tea, I'll eat at the canteen.

> GEORGE *exits.* HELEN *enters and signals* CAMPBELL *to follow her. He obeys.*

MARK	*Rotterdam*'s just cleared the dock, it's making for the pass.
MATTHEW	Wish I was on it.
MARK	Wish I was driving it.

> CAMPBELL *enters on the roof.*

CAMPBELL Hey. He's gone. Back to the station. Your mother wants you downstairs for your tea.

MATTHEW You heard what he said: "No tea or dinner."

MARK C'mon, I'm starving.

MATTHEW Go, if you like. I'm staying here.

MARK Suit yourself.

> MARK *exits.*

CAMPBELL You didn't tell on me—why?

MATTHEW He wanted me to. I won't give him the satisfaction.

CAMPBELL *Dor ger, die gor.* [Thank you] .

> MATTHEW *and* CAMPBELL *look at each other.* HELEN *enters on the roof. She places her hand on* CAMPBELL'*s arm.* CAMPBELL *exits.*

HELEN Matthew, there's shrimp on toast.

MATTHEW "No tea or dinner." Isn't that what he said?

> MATTHEW *faces away from* HELEN. HELEN *stands beside* MATTHEW. *They both look out towards the harbour.*

MATTHEW I hate him.

HELEN You must not talk like that.

MATTHEW He picks on me, can't you see that?

> *They are silent for a moment.*

HELEN He wants your respect.

MATTHEW   My respect? Ha!

HELEN   *(gently)* Yes, just a little more respect from his eldest son.... All his life he has had to fight for respect... he's had a hard life... many disappointments....

MATTHEW   I know the story, he had to sacrifice law school because he had to support a family, da-da-da-da-da....

HELEN   Yes, but that's not all.... Matthew, if you try to understand why he is like he is, then maybe you won't feel the need to be disrespectful of his wishes.

MATTHEW   Why? Why must I be the one to "understand"?

HELEN   Because you are the stronger....

                A moment.

                My family didn't respect him.... He was from Shanghai.... we are Hong Kong people for four generations.... He fought against the Japs and was a prisoner of war for three years, but the British government doesn't seem to care about his contribution.... In '49 he went home to Shanghai to rescue his grandmother, who was jailed by the commies. They jailed him too, and confiscated their property.

                He has nothing to give you and that frustrates him.... He needs our understanding and support—if not from my family, or from the British, or even the commies, then at least from his wife and children....

                A moment.

MATTHEW   And that's what you do?

HELEN   It's for the best.

MATTHEW	You hold your tongue, respectfully.
HELEN	He has been a loyal husband and father.
MATTHEW	You are asking me to show him respect. How can I, when he doesn't respect me?
HELEN	You'll understand better one day.
MATTHEW	That day is now. And you know, Mama, I still don't understand.

> *MATTHEW exits. HELEN stares out toward the harbour for a long moment. Meanwhile, the final musical strains of a Catholic High Mass are heard. MARK enters, dressed as an altar boy and carrying an incense burner. Once "off" the altar area, he swings the incense burner like a hammer toss. HELEN exits.*

CAMPBELL	Have you got it?
MARK	Huh?
CAMPBELL	You chickened out.
MARK	No, I didn't. I have it here.
CAMPBELL	Let's see it, let's see it.
MARK	Here?
CAMPBELL	The priests never come through here.
MARK	I know, but—
CAMPBELL	Chicken.
MARK	You're a chicken.... OK, here....

> *MARK reaches inside his cassock, and takes out something wrapped in a handkerchief.*

MARK	We should wait for Matthew.
CAMPBELL	He has cricket practice. I want to try it now.

> CAMPBELL *takes the handkerchief, and unwraps it to reveal a communion wafer. Meanwhile,* MARK *is changing out of his cassock.*

Wow! How did you get—

MARK	Shhh! Before the Offertory, I slipped one out of the chalice.
CAMPBELL	If you hold it up to the light, you can see the inside of his body.

> CAMPBELL *covers his fingers with the handkerchief and holds up the communion wafer. He holds it up to the light. They both stare at it.*

MARK	I don't see anything.
CAMPBELL	Me neither. Maybe it has to be consecrated first.
MARK	Only priests can do that.
CAMPBELL	Anyone can do it.
MARK	No, they can't.
CAMPBELL	Priests are men, just like us. Why are they the only ones allowed to use those magic words?
MARK	Holy words.

> MARK *covers the wafer with the handkerchief.*

CAMPBELL	Let's do it.
MARK	What?

CAMPBELL   The consecration.

MARK   We can't do that.

CAMPBELL   Why not?

MARK   Because... only priests can.

CAMPBELL   That's just another way they have of putting
             themselves above the people.

MARK   It's a sin.

CAMPBELL   Seven "Our Fathers" penance—maximum.

                    CAMPBELL *pulls the wafer out.*

MARK   We should wait for Matthew.

CAMPBELL   C'mon, don't you want to find out if this really
             turns into the body and blood of—

MARK   Don't say it!

CAMPBELL   I'm going to do it.

MARK   No, you mustn't.

                    CAMPBELL *closes his eyes, summons
                    his spirituality, leans solemnly over the
                    wafer, and pronounces each word very
                    deliberately and with complete sincerity.*

CAMPBELL   *Hoc... est... Corpus... Christi....*

             Bells.

MARK   What?

CAMPBELL   Ring the bells.

                    MARK *instinctively reaches to his left,
                    and mimes the ringing of a bell.*

MARK	Ring, ring, ring. Ring, ring, ring.
	CAMPBELL *lowers the wafer. A moment.*
CAMPBELL	There, it's done.... Oh... oh... oh, my gosh... I think I see something... oh, my gosh... it's....
MARK	What? What do you see?
CAMPBELL	There are veins, they're blue... and its turning red.... Oh, no... all that blood... what's that? A heart...? I think I see... a heart....
MARK	A heart?
CAMPBELL	Yes... throbbing... boom-boom, boom-boom—
MARK	Let me see!
CAMPBELL	Careful! You'll break it and it will bleed all over! Now... carefully, carefully... a little closer, closer.... Now, lean in and... see?
MARK	I don't see anything.
CAMPBELL	Oh, it's gone.
MARK	Liar.
CAMPBELL	Let's eat it.
MARK	What?
CAMPBELL	I'll break it in half and we'll share it.
MARK	No! Don't do that!
CAMPBELL	Why not? Afraid it'll bleed when I break it? Afraid you'll taste the blood in your mouth? Well, here goes....
	CAMPBELL *bends the wafer slowly, slowly, until—snap—it breaks.*

CAMPBELL	Aah!
MARK	Aah!
CAMPBELL	No blood, it's OK, it's OK.... Phew! See, no problem.
MARK	Phew...! What now?
CAMPBELL	Here, this half's yours.
MARK	What am I going to do with it?
CAMPBELL	Eat it.
MARK	Are you crazy?
CAMPBELL	Nothing will happen.
MARK	Oh, no?
CAMPBELL	No.
MARK	Then, *you* eat it.
CAMPBELL	OK, I will....

> CAMPBELL *first puts one half into his mouth like a fire-eater would. He looks at* MARK. *No problem. He puts the second half in his mouth. He looks at* MARK.

There!

> *He chews, swallows, then burps.*

Told you nothing would happen.

> CAMPBELL *suddenly stiffens, his face reddens.*

MARK	Campbell, are you alright?

> CAMPBELL *clutches his own throat,*
> *doubles over in pain, collapses to the*
> *ground, tries to open his collar....*

MARK Campbell... Campbell.... What's the matter...?
What's happening...? Oh God, oh God....

> CAMPBELL *points frantically to his*
> *mouth.*

What? What do you want me to do? What should I
do? What should I do?

> CAMPBELL*'s signals get weaker.*

Breathe! You can't breathe? No? Drink? You want
something to drink? Oh my God, oh my God....

> CAMPBELL *grabs* MARK*'s shoulder,*
> *pulls himself up to eye level, his face*
> *contorted in agony.*

Oh my God, oh my God....

> *When they are nose-to-nose,*
> CAMPBELL*'s face returns to normal.*

CAMPBELL *(flatly)* There is no God.

MARK What?

> CAMPBELL *roars with laughter.* MARK
> *is upset.*

You bum!

CAMPBELL Boom-boom, boom-boom— Aaaah, you should see
your face.... Hooooo, good one.

MARK You... bum....

CAMPBELL Wait 'till I tell Matthew, he'll be sorry he
missed—

> SARAH WOTFORD *enters behind*
> MARK. *She stands at the entrance of the*
> *change room.*

CAMPBELL   *Neigh geh nui pung yao ah.* [Your girlfriend.]

SARAH   Speak English.

CAMPBELL   *Neigh gui kui jiao la, ngor day yew hui geen neigh*
             gor die gor wan "cricket" nah. [Tell her to go away,
             and let's go watch your brother's cricket practice.]

SARAH   What did he say about cricket?

MARK   Nothing.

CAMPBELL   Ha-lo, goo-by!

SARAH   Mark, I waited and waited—

CAMPBELL   Waiting for her boyfriend, la la la la la la....

> SARAH *glares at him.*

SARAH   Mark?

CAMPBELL   Haaaa, the tigress awakens!

MARK   Shut up.

SARAH   Who is he, anyway?

MARK   He's just the houseboy.

SARAH   Cheeky, isn't he?

MARK   *(to* CAMPBELL*)* Don't you look at me like that.

CAMPBELL   No girls allowed in here.

SARAH   What's he on about?

MARK   *(to* CAMPBELL*)* Don't be cheeky—

CAMPBELL   *Hui lah, mm-sai tung kui gong lah....* [Let's go, you don't have to talk to her.]

SARAH   What's he saying? What are you saying?

MARK   I'll tell my father about—you know what—and then you'll be out on your arse. Savvy?

CAMPBELL   Yes.

MARK   "Yes" what?

CAMPBELL   Yes, sir.

> CAMPBELL *picks* MARK*'s cassock off the floor.* MARK *and* SARAH *exit.*

All for one and one for all—huh!

> MARK *enters on the roof.* CAMPBELL *exits.*

MARK   Give me your hand.

> *He pulls* SARAH *up.*

SARAH   So, this is your "secret place." It's so open.

MARK   Aaah, but you can only get here by the fire escape.

SARAH   I was thinking it would be... different.

> *He places a hand over her eyes.*

Hey!

MARK   Step over here.

> *He leads her downstage.*

OK, ready?

SARAH   What for?

MARK	This.
	He removes his hand.
	Isn't it fab?
SARAH	What?
MARK	The harbour... the ships... Lion Rock.
SARAH	You can see my place. Over there. The army barracks, and beside it—demonstrators!
MARK	Where?
SARAH	Seems there's more of them everyday. *(shouting)* Go home, this is British territory, not China! Commies! Me dad says if they let him take his troops to them, it'd all be over in minutes....
	SARAH *looks over the edge.*
SARAH	Quite a drop.
MARK	Eight floors. You can leap from roof to roof, almost to the other side of the city.
SARAH	Do you bring all your girlfriends up here?
MARK	Not all... some... a few. You're the first. Only my brother, me, and you know about it—and Campbell.
SARAH	He's from the Resettlements, isn't he?
MARK	Yes. My parents took him in and gave him a job....
SARAH	Well, he should be grateful.
	Pause.
MARK	Hey, I want to show you something.

MARK *pulls out his notebook.*

SARAH   What is it?

MARK   Take a look.

SARAH   Oh, this is what you were telling me about.

MARK   It's a journal of those ships over there—here, let me show you. Date, the beginning of the week, then here— name: *Queen of the North.* That's the white one over there.

SARAH   With the two funnels?

MARK   That's right.

SARAH   It's big.

MARK   Sixty-four thousand tons. Registration: Holland. Eighteen-hundred passenger capacity....

SARAH   What's that one with the cranes?

MARK   That's the... let's see... ah, the *Singapore Maru.* Registration: Panama. Twelve thousand tons. One-hundred and fifty passenger capacity.

SARAH   And... that one?

MARK   That would be... red and white with blue stripe... the *SS Mary Bell.* Registration: UK....

SARAH   Let me guess. Three hundred passengers.

MARK   Four hundred and fifty capacity.

SARAH   But it looks smaller than the *Singapore Maru.*

MARK	The *Mary Bell* is a passenger liner and the *Maru* is more of a cargo ship. See—when they arrive, when they weigh anchor, where they are headed for, and their lading. My brother says we are going to hop aboard one day and get away from here, maybe to America.
SARAH	What are you going to be when you leave school?
MARK	I've told you.
SARAH	Tell me again.
MARK	I'm going to captain one of those and sail the world: Oahu, San Francisco, Managua, Trujillo, Valparaiso, Montevideo, Rio de Janeiro....
SARAH	Will you take me?
MARK	I thought you were going to write novels in Paris.
SARAH	Paris... wherever. Just think. You a sailor—
MARK	Captain—
SARAH	And me a famous novelist—hey, I just thought of something. Romeo and Juliet. Your parents don't know about me, and my parents don't know about you, and we meet on your "balcony"—that part is a bit different, but it's high up and away from the street. And you've got this creepy friend who's like Mercutio—they're both a bit potty, laughing and falling about in the middle of the road, and... and... and you're a Catholic and I'm Protestant.
	"Romeo, Romeo, wherefore art thou Romeo Deny thy father and refuse thy name Or if thou wilt not be but sworn my love And I'll no longer be a Capulet...."
MARK	Romeo and Juliet were both Catholics.
SARAH	They were?

MARK	Have you ever seen an Italian who wasn't Catholic?
SARAH	Romeo and Juliet were Italian?
MARK	Verona? Italy?
SARAH	Isn't that funny. I knew that—I mean, I thought I knew that, I must have known that. You know, you just don't think of people except how you think they should be. Campbell's Chinese, I'm English, and you're... where are you from, I never asked.
MARK	Oh... our people came from Dunfree....
SARAH	Where?
MARK	It's in Scotland.
SARAH	Oh, you mean Dumfries. *(pronounced "Dumfreeze")*
MARK	Yes, that's right.... Um... I read your short story. Actually, I read it twice... no... yes, twice, and....
SARAH	And you hated it.
MARK	Why do you say that?
SARAH	You said you'd tell me today what you thought of it, and we've been up here for hours and you haven't said a thing. Go ahead, you can tell me.

She squeezes her eyes shut.

SARAH	Anais Nin said: "Artists must learn to steel themselves against the lances of disappointment."
MARK	Well....
SARAH	The editor of the *South China Morning Post* will thank you for having to read one less entry for the Short Story Contest.

MARK   It's not that I didn't like it... it's, well, frankly, it's a bit... different.

One eye opens.

It's about me—someone like me—and someone like... you....

Both eyes open, eager.

And they....

SARAH   Make mad, passionate love at their "secret place," freely, innocently....

MARK   Take this passage: "Lost in the mist which surrounded her like an endless white cloak, she stumbled on the uneven ground of the moors. Looking up, she saw him standing over her. A black wisp of hair from the thick mane on his head, had fallen on his smooth brow, framing one side of his face. His eyes were as dark, as rich and as deep, as a barrel of chocolate. Standing there, he seemed to her like an exotic prince on the misty Hong Kong Moors...."

She moves close to him.

SARAH   You have deep, chocolate eyes. That's what I noticed about you when we first met, at the pictures....

Closer.

What did you notice about me...?
A breath away.

MARK   I... I forget....

SARAH   It was only two weeks, three days, and four hours ago....

Touching his eyebrow.

SARAH   One of them is almond shaped....

Almost a kiss, when they hear
CAMPBELL *offstage:*

CAMPBELL   *Yee goon! Yee goon ah! Neigh high seung been mah?* [Second son, second son, are you up there?]

MARK   *High see ah! Joe mutt yeah ah?* [I'm here. What's up?]

SARAH   You speak Chinee!

MARK   Um... a few words....

SARAH   Wow, that's amazing. Where did you learn? Say something for me....

CAMPBELL *enters.*

CAMPBELL   *Jeow lah.* [Let's go.]

MARK   Must dash.

MARK *starts to exit.*

SARAH   Coming to the dance, Saturday?

MARK   Dance?

SARAH   You remember, in the caff, it's for all the teens in the barracks? We get to hear all the latest records from home.

MARK   Um....

SARAH   It's only five dollars. Please come, I want you to meet all me friends.

MARK   Um....

CAMPBELL   C'mon, they're in the car waiting.

MARK   There are no "moors" in Hong Kong.

> MARK *exits. Music.* CAMPBELL *and* SARAH *look at each other. Music and Chinese New Year firecrackers explode.* CAMPBELL *does a strutting Chinese dance.* SARAH *turns and exits.*
>
> *Then, a giant portrait appears, of a Chinese woman wearing traditional Chinese gown. The* SIMMONS *family enter and stand in a row, smiling, except for* MATTHEW *who has his arms folded.* CAMPBELL *joins them.*

HELEN   *Gung Hey Faaht Choy!* [Happy New Year]

GEORGE   *Gung Hey Faaht Choy!*

MARK   *Gung Hey Faaht Choy!*

CAMPBELL   *Gung Hey Faaht Choy!*

> *A shower of red "lai see" packets fall from the sky.* MARK *and* CAMPBELL *rush to pick them up and stuff them into their pockets. The family crosses to their home.* HELEN *is studying a list. Music fades.*

HELEN   The Wongs, Older Ho, Younger Ho, the Chows....

MARK   This one's from third aunt? Guess how much.

CAMPBELL   Five dollars.

> MARK *and* CAMPBELL *look inside the packet.*

BOTH   One dollar.

MARK   What a stinge.

HELEN   Mark, that's no way to talk. She does the best she can.

MARK   Hey, Matthew, open yours.

MATTHEW	Later.
MARK	OK, but I'm opening mine now.
GEORGE .	Stayed far too long at the Lees, I think.
HELEN	Well, it was you and your brandy.
GEORGE	Me? What about your mah-jong game?
HELEN	We'll have to move Auntie May-ling to tomorrow's list.
MARK	Is she Grandfather's last concubine?

> HELEN *taps* MARK *on the head.*

Ow.

HELEN	You ask me that every year.
GEORGE	Your mother looked well.
HELEN	Yes. She seems in very good spirits.
GEORGE	It's the one day she is civil to me.
HELEN	Well, it's New Year, time to forget problems and think of the future.
GEORGE	Let's not get too comfortable, those commies are lulling Hong Kong into a false sense of confidence. You mark my words—
HELEN	Oh, George, let's not think about that today.
GEORGE	You're right. Oh, my feet. I'm all in. When's dinner?
HELEN	I'll get some sandwiches. Campbell, Mark, Matthew?
CAMPBELL	Yes, ma'am.

HELEN	I'm very proud of you boys.
GEORGE	Yes, you did well.
HELEN	Remembering everyone's Chinese name and rank.
MARK	"*Gung Hey Faaht Choy* [Happy New Year], Third Great Aunt, younger than my maternal grandmother."

He imitates her voice, and the giving of a "lai see":

"*Gung Hei Faaht Choy.*"

HELEN and CAMPBELL cover their smiles. Even GEORGE enjoys the charade.

| GEORGE | He's such an actor. |
| MARK | *Dor ger.* [Thank you.] |

Takes a "lai see" from his pocket and looks in it.

Wow! Ten dollars. I like her.

HELEN	I'll take that.
GEORGE	Even I get all mixed up with the old aunts and uncles.
MARK	"Happy New Year, Second Great Uncle, younger than my paternal great-grandfather."

He acts out another relative:

"Have you been a good boy?" "Yes, Great Uncle." "Are you sure?" "Yes, Great Uncle." "Well, because you're so sure, you can have two!" "*Dor ger.*" [Thank you]

He opens the envelope.

CAMPBELL	Ha! That's good.
GEORGE	*(warning)* Hey!
MARK	Twenty dollars!! I like him best so far.
HELEN	I'll take that. Matthew, may I have your *lai see foong* please. You too, Mark.

MATTHEW *and* MARK *hand them in.*

MARK	Can I have five dollars?
HELEN	What for?
MARK	Ice cream.
HELEN	In February? Behave yourself.... All of them.

MARK *takes one envelope from his sock.*

Thank you.

GEORGE	Look, boys, we keep that money every year for your future. With all the commie trouble, we may have to get you both out of here quickly. Without passports, the money will help.
HELEN	This is also for your education—
GEORGE	Yes, yes. You see, boys, I had to quit law school to raise this family—that's why I joined the police. If I couldn't be a lawyer, then I could at least be the law. If I'm tough on you, its only because I know what's best. The thing of it is, your mother and I want you to have a better chance. Better than I had. You need a good education.... Aaah, I'm tired, and a little tipsy, and you've heard it all before....
HELEN	Campbell, my mother gave me this to give to you. For a rainy day.

She gives him a "lai see." MARK watches.

CAMPBELL   *Dor ger, tai-tai.* [Thank you, ma'am.]

GEORGE   Alright, let's get washed for dinner, then bed. We'll have to start early tomorrow if we want to get through that list. And no mah-jong.

HELEN   And no brandy. Campbell, help me with the tea.

MATTHEW   I'm not going.

GEORGE   Don't be silly.

MARK   If I have to wash my hands, he has to too.

MATTHEW   Shuttup, Mark. I'm not going to do anymore visits tomorrow.

HELEN   But it's tradition, everybody goes visiting on Chinese New Year—

MATTHEW   Not "everybody."

GEORGE   Wuzzat?

MATTHEW   Why do we have to do this?

GEORGE   This is something you will understand when you are older. Now, stop this bloody nonsense—

MATTHEW   It's not bloody nonsense—

GEORGE   Wuzzat?

MATTHEW   I said it's not bloody nonsense!

GEORGE   Don't you raise your voice to me, boy.

MATTHEW   I'm a man, I can decide for myself—

GEORGE   You're not too old to get six of the best.

          Beat.

Alright. We'll talk about it in the morning.

MATTHEW	I'm not going in the morning, in the afternoon, not ever.
GEORGE	I said, we'll discuss it in the morning.
MATTHEW	No.
GEORGE	What?
HELEN	Tomorrow's list are cousins and old family friends. It's not essential for Matthew. We can say he's not feeling well, it doesn't matter—
GEORGE	Of course it matters—that would be lying, and we are not going to commit a venial sin because of this ungrateful boy.
HELEN	(*to* MATTHEW*)* It will just be a couple of hours, it'll be over before you know it. It means so much to—
MATTHEW	(*to* GEORGE*)* I don't even know all their names or how we are related to them, and we go every year, dressed in our Sunday best, and stand around smiling, half choking from the stink of joss sticks, and drinking endless cups of tea, and then they give us little packets of money, and you have to give them little packets of money—which you can't afford to do.... It's all so humiliating....

HELEN *plays with her ring, nervously.*

GEORGE	These are traditions—
MATTHEW	They are Chinese traditions, and I am English. You said so—and so, why don't we behave like it?
GEORGE	How dare you.
HELEN	Matthew, apologize.
MATTHEW	No. It's the truth. I'm not going to lie. Explain it to me. See, you can't. You say one thing, and then do another. That's hypocrisy.

GEORGE   That's enough. Six of the best. Get in there—both of you.

MARK   That's not fair.

MATTHEW   He didn't do anything.

GEORGE   It's for the future. In case he gets any funny ideas.

MATTHEW   Leave him out of it. I'll take his share.

GEORGE   In that case, you get double.

MATTHEW   You can hit me as much as you like, but I swear, you will regret this for the rest of your life.

GEORGE   Get in there—now!

> GEORGE *pushes* MATTHEW *offstage.* HELEN *gathers up the "lai see" money and wraps it in a large handkerchief.*
>
> *After a few moments,* GEORGE *pushes* MATTHEW *onstage.*

That hurt me more than it hurt you.

HELEN   I'll get dinner ready.

GEORGE   No dinner. Bed.

> GEORGE *exits.* HELEN *looks at the boys.*

HELEN   Goodnight, boys.

MARK   Goodnight, Mother.

> HELEN *exits with the money wrapped in a handkerchief. The boys all stare at* CAMPBELL's *"lai see" envelope.*

MATTHEW   Let me tell you something. To the Hindu *fakir*, who can sit for hours on a couch of nails, overcoming pain by mental discipline is a sign of spiritual growth and understanding. Pain is not really "felt" on the palm of the hands, or on the backside, or on the cheeks—no, it's all inside the head, in the thalamus and the cerebral cortex, to be exact. Although some may argue that pain is due to defects in moral character, an imbalance of the Ying and Yang. Some others maintain that the English word "pain" has its Latin roots in the word "penalty" and therefore, if you feel it, you must deserve it.

But I know that pain is really contained in a tiny, little, microscopic part, deep in here. And this little thing sends electrical, chemical, and biological signals to some of the fifteen billion nerves and neurons which make you think you feel pain here, and here, and here. So, if I can, mentally, isolate that tiny, microscopic, spot in the brain, and concentrate very hard, I can make that tiny spot numb, and by doing that, I don't feel any pain. I have trained myself to do that. So, I don't ever feel any physical pain. But the hurt in here.... requires action.

> MATTHEW *exits.* MARK *snatches the "lai see" from* CAMPBELL.

CAMPBELL   Hey!

MARK   I need it.

CAMPBELL   What for?

MARK   Never you mind.

> CAMPBELL *snatches the "lai see" out of* MARK*'s hand.*

CAMPBELL   Why do you go with the English girl? She is playing with you. When trouble comes, the army will leave, and she too.

MARK   I'll pay you back.

CAMPBELL   You should find a local girl, because you are a local
                boy. Why do you have to pretend?

MARK   I'll tell my father about the firecrackers.

CAMPBELL   Yes, then we all will be punished....

MARK   But you will lose your job here, and be out on the
                street....

                          Pause.
CAMPBELL   I see....

MARK   I'll pay it back....

CAMPBELL   Here....

MARK   I'll pay it back. Promise.

                MARK *exits.* CAMPBELL *remains
                onstage.*

                *The lights fade. Very loud rock music
                plays, circa 1967.* CAMPBELL *hides and
                watches as* MARK *enters with* SARAH.
                They are jiving. MARK *becomes more
                and more frantic....*

SARAH   Ow... don't... Mark, you're hurting me... ow...
                stop it, people are watching... stop it... stop it....
                Where are you going? Mark....

                He goes "outside."

                For Pete's sake....

                She joins him "outside."

                Can I have a cigarette?

> *She waits for a response. Getting none, she plucks an "air" cigarette from his direction.*

SARAH   Ta.

> *She looks at the cigarette, looks at him, looks at the cigarette, then looks at him.*

Got a light?

> *She lights her cigarette with an "air" lighter.*

Ta again.... You're very welcome, Sarah.... My, you've got a pretty dress on this eve', is it new? Why, yeah, I got it on Portebello Road before comin' over. You don't think it's too short? No, not at all, I fancy a bit of leg in me girlfriends.... What's the matter, Markus? You are so...

MARK   I just wish they wouldn't talk about "back home in England this, in England that"—who cares?

SARAH   ...uptight.

MARK   Uptight?

SARAH   Yeah, you know—twitchy....

MARK   Twitchy.

SARAH   If you repeat everything I say, I might as well talk to myself.

> *She waits for a response.*

Me friends think you're ever so mysterious, and Jane's just green.... You're a good dancer, except for that last one.... Do you like "Rubber Soul"? My fav's "You Won't See Me."

She sings:

SARAH	"When I call you up, your line's engaged I have had enough, so act your age We have lost the dime That was so hard to find And I will lose my mind If you won't see me, You won't see me You won't see me You won't see me Well, I know—"
MARK	"Time"
SARAH	Huh? Ah... nine-thirty.
MARK	It's "time," not "dime." "We have lost the time, that was so hard to find...."
SARAH	You sure? "We have lost the time... we have lost the dime...." You sure?
MARK	Positive.
SARAH	Doesn't matter, but I do think a dime is easier to find than time.
MARK	It won't make any sense if you use "dime." They are talking about losing the great time they once shared and now she won't see him....
SARAH	Who?
MARK	They—him—the singer. They—I mean he—wouldn't be talking about a dime that was lost—
SARAH	Why not?
MARK	Well, because they didn't lose any dimes, they have lost time which they—or rather he—spent with her at one time....

SARAH   What if they had a lucky dime, which was like a good luck charm, and he lost it—

MARK   Don't be a git. That doesn't make any sense—

SARAH   It makes sense to me—

MARK   How? How can it possibly make sense?

SARAH   I got you talking.

> *A moment.*

Oh, oh, oh, I see a teeny, little smile....

> *The music changes to a slow tune.*
> SARAH *takes his hands and places them on her waist, then puts her arms around his neck.*

OK?

> *With their foreheads touching, they sway to the slow rhythm.* CAMPBELL *enters in the shadows and watches them.*

MARK   Sarah, I want to tell you something... about me....

SARAH   Yes?

MARK   You see, I'm—

SARAH   You don't have to. I know.

MARK   How do you know?

SARAH   A woman's intuition.... Anais says: "Showing is always more complete than telling...."

> *She kisses him on the mouth.* MARK *runs off.*

Mark! Mark!

> *She runs after him.* MARK *reappears in a different area and stops, panting.*

CAMPBELL   Sssst.

MARK   Campbell?

CAMPBELL   Over here, she will see.

SARAH   Mark! Come back....

> *They crouch down to hide.* SARAH *crosses and exits.*

CAMPBELL   She's gone. See!

MARK   What are you doing here?

CAMPBELL   I'm your guardian angel.

MARK   Silly git.

CAMPBELL   What happened?

MARK   Nothing.

CAMPBELL   Did she say something...? Do something...?

MARK   No....

CAMPBELL   Then why were you running from her?

MARK   I wasn't running from her.

CAMPBELL   You don't like her anymore.

MARK   No— Yes— It's not her... it's the others, in the caff....

CAMPBELL   *Sik duck harm yue, dai duck hart.*

MARK   What?

CAMPBELL   "If you eat salt fish, be prepared for thirst...." If you want to mix with them, you have to be one of them.... Better to stay with Hong Kong girls. Be proud of your Chinese roots. The face of Hong Kong may be British, but its heart and soul is Chinese. Just like you. You may look European, but inside, you are Chinese.

MARK *starts to leave.*

Hear me out, you owe me that much.

MARK *stays.*

Chinese girls will like you. They will understand you.... But going out with girls is expensive. You have to pay for everything.

MARK   I'll manage.

CAMPBELL   How? You borrowed five dollars for tonight.

MARK   I'll pay you back, next week....

CAMPBELL   How? Your parents never give you pocket money, your clothes are bought from the *"lay yeung guy"*—the street stalls where you get cheap things, not like the other boys who have all their clothes tailor made—

MARK *starts to leave.*

Wait— You need money, we both need money, and I know how to get some.... Look....

CAMPBELL *takes out a little box.*

CAMPBELL   Come, I want to show you something. Come, it won't bite.... Take it.

MARK   A "Dinky Toy"

CAMPBELL   Look inside.

MARK   A "Rolls."

CAMPBELL   "Silver Shadow." Guess how much.

MARK   Two fifty.

CAMPBELL   Three seventy-five. "Rolls" cost more.

MARK   It's a beaut.

CAMPBELL   I give to you.

MARK   No— I—

CAMPBELL   Take it. I am your friend....

MARK   I already owe you five dollars....

Pause.

CAMPBELL   You like to *make* some money?

MARK   How?

CAMPBELL   This car, I can sell for two dollar. See?

MARK   You just *lost* money.

CAMPBELL   But I got this car for nothing.

MARK   Where?

CAMPBELL   From that little shop, behind the post office. I just go in and....

He pinches his thumb and index finger together.

MARK   You pinched it.

CAMPBELL   What is "pinched"?

MARK   You nicked... you stole it.

CAMPBELL   I liberated the toy.... You can do it, too.

MARK   No, I don't think so. I don't steal things.

CAMPBELL   You have before.

MARK   When?

CAMPBELL   My five dollars.

MARK   You loaned it to me—

CAMPBELL   And you can't pay me back.... You used it for the dance, no? Yes, you did, and I agree with that, money should be spread around equally, no one should have more money than his neighbour....

MARK   Look, I'll pay you back—

CAMPBELL   How? How are you going to get it...? Do you have any *lai see* money? In my way, you can make some money, no one will know, not even Matthew, only you and me....

MARK   I don't know, it's—

CAMPBELL   A sin? Look, over here, see? Read that.

MARK   "Made in Hong Kong."

CAMPBELL   You know those factories on Kowloon side? The workers there make these for the *say gweilo die bahn*, maybe twenty cents each, and the shops here sell them for three dollar seventy-five—that is a sin, my friend.

A moment.

They steal from us, we have to take back what is ours—come, I show you, very easy to do—

Lights change to the "shop."

The shop is small....

MARK	I know the one....
CAMPBELL	Good, good. You go in....

A bell tinkles, traffic noise.

And you have to close the door....

Traffic noise is muted.

Immediately in front of you is the counter and cash register, where that bastard, Sinden, sits reading the racing forms. He is too stupid to see anything. The shop is L-shaped, bending to his right and away from him to the back of the shop. The "Dinky" and "Matchbox" sections are farthest away from him. He looks up. You smile and nod. He nods at you and goes back to his racing forms.

MARK	Where are you?
CAMPBELL	Behind you.
MARK	Why am I in front?
CAMPBELL	Because you look like a *gweilo* and he won't suspect.
MARK	Am I wearing my blazer?
CAMPBELL	Yes, everything is normal, like you dropped in after school....
MARK	OK—then?
CAMPBELL	Then we look around at the comics in the front section. Casual, casual, nothing wrong, nothing unusual. We make a few comments to each other about the current issues. Then, I stay in the front section reading, while you go towards the back—
MARK	Me? Why me?

CAMPBELL	Ssssh. You go towards the back, but you don't go straight there. You look along the walls, you look interested in the items on the shelves, and wander slowly to the back....
	(in Sinden's voice) Can I help you find something?
MARK	Huh? Uh... no... just looking, thanks....
CAMPBELL	Good, good—
MARK	Don't do that—
CAMPBELL	You keep walking to the back, casual, casual, maybe you stop on the way, pick up an item and look at it, then move on, closer and closer to your target. Finally, you are there. In front of you is a whole wall of "Dinkys" and "Matchboxes." Rolls are on top. They have a little dust on them, so don't sneeze, too expensive unless you are a *gweilo*. Then the Jags, then the Aston Martins, and so on down to the Morris cars at the bottom.
MARK	I know, I've seen them—
CAMPBELL	Ssssh.... You take two and put them in your inside pocket, two more in each pants pocket, and two more in your bag....
MARK	What, what's happening?
CAMPBELL	Ssssh.... Sinden looks up, he is seeing only me.... He is getting up from his stool and is about to come around the corner to see where you are.
MARK	What do I do?
CAMPBELL	Don't panic.
MARK	What do I do? Put them back?
CAMPBELL	No, you stay there.
MARK	He's coming.

CAMPBELL   "I would like to buy this, sir."

                      Pause.

MARK   What's happening, what's happening?

CAMPBELL   I am holding a "Superman" and a "Batman." He looks at me. He looks at the comics. He leans towards the back to see if he can see you.... "Can I have them in a paper bag please, sir?" He takes the comics from me. He is not sure if he should go look for you at the back or not. But he can't turn away a sale. He returns to the cash to ring it up. "Ching." One dollar and twenty cents—that is your signal.

MARK   What is?

CAMPBELL   The bell. "Ching."

MARK   What for?

                      Lights are restored to "normal" night.

CAMPBELL   *Neigh geh mong ding ah!* [You idiot!] To leave, of course. You do so quickly. I pay for the comics and follow you out. Then we meet, and I give you two dollars for each car.

MARK   How can I trust you? You are a houseboy. For years you have been a servant, but I know nothing about you.

                      Pause.

CAMPBELL   Ask me.

                      Pause.

MARK   What?

CAMPBELL   Where do I come from? I don't know.... Who are
my parents? I don't know. All I know is they didn't
want me.... Orphanage... it's like a jail for short
people... I learned to survive very quickly.... Nuns,
religion... they gave me this stupid name because
Campbell soup gave them a donation.... They got
rid of me by putting me in foster homes....

Finally, two years ago, the St. Stephen's Society
picked me for sponsorship to your school. Your
father became my godfather... but to earn my way I
had to become the houseboy.... I have no family....

An awkward pause.

MARK   Eight dollars. What if I have more?

CAMPBELL   You like money, huh? OK, we skip one day and go
the next day.

MARK   I thought you boys in the "D" stream were
dummies.

CAMPBELL   Go. Tomorrow we get rich.... Friends...?

> CAMPBELL *and* MARK *lock eyes, and*
> CAMPBELL *touches* MARK's *eyebrow.*
> MARK *exits. Lights up on the*
> SIMMONS *apartment, where* MATTHEW
> *finishes writing a letter.* MARK *is in his*
> *own bed.* MATTHEW *enters the bedroom.*
> *A clock chimes.* CAMPBELL *exits.*

MATTHEW   Mark... Mark....

MARK   Huh? What time is it?

MATTHEW   Ssssh. You'll wake the others.

MARK   Is it time to get up?

MATTHEW   No, not for a couple of hours.... I'm leaving....

MARK   For school? It's too early....

MATTHEW	No.... It's time for action.... There's a steamer sailing with the tide at six thirty-one... you know the one....
MARK	Where—?
MATTHEW	America on the—
MARK	*Pacific Maru*—
MATTHEW	Right. Tonnage?
MARK	Twelve thousand, carries six passengers—
MATTHEW	They're going to let me sign on as a clerk. And because I have my "O" levels, I didn't have to pay as much to join.
MARK	Where did you get the money ?

A beat.

MATTHEW	Campbell says you have a girlfriend.
MARK	I won't take her to the roof again.
MATTHEW	It's OK, you can take her there if you want. What's her name?
MARK	Sarah.
MATTHEW	How did you meet her?
MARK	At the school matinee for "The Sound of Music." Her school sat in front of ours. She kept waving at me.... When are you coming back?

> MATTHEW *peels a bank note from a wad wrapped in a handkerchief.*

MATTHEW	Here, buy her some flowers, girls like that.... I must go—
MARK	Why?

MATTHEW	I can't be here anymore, I just can't. It's all in this letter. I'll leave it on the table, it explains everything. I'll write when I get settled. You'll understand one day. It's easier for you than me. I'm the eldest.... Hey, hey, don't do that.... Look, promise you won't tell anyone until at least nine a.m.—
HELEN	*(off)* Campbell! Campbell!
CAMPBELL	*(off)* Coming, ma'am.
MATTHEW	Shit!
MARK	What's going on?
MATTHEW	You musn't say anything until nine a.m. Promise.

HELEN *enters the dining room.*

HELEN	Did you lock all the doors last night?
MATTHEW	Promise.
CAMPBELL	Yes, ma'am.
MATTHEW	Mark.
HELEN	Check them.
CAMPBELL	*(off)* Yes, ma'am.
MARK	I promise.
GEORGE	Boys! Boys, wake up, wake up. The doors?
HELEN	He's checking them.
GEORGE	The windows are all closed and locked.

MATTHEW *and* MARK *enter the dining room.*

MATTHEW	What's the matter?

CAMPBELL   The door is locked, just as I left it, ma'am.

GEORGE   We've been robbed, boys.

HELEN   All the cash I put in the drawer.

GEORGE   Several hundred dollars.

HELEN   For emergencies, in case we had to leave quickly.

GEORGE   No one came in here, so it must have been—

HELEN   NO!

GEORGE   Right, let's have a look, then.

> GEORGE *exits to* CAMPBELL*'s room,
> while the others wait in silence. Finally:*

(off) Goddammit!

> GEORGE *enters carrying a shoebox which
> he empties on the table. "Dinky Toy" cars
> tumble out.*

I didn't have to go far. Where did these come from?

HELEN   Campbell?

GEORGE   Under his bed.

HELEN   Campbell?

GEORGE   Have you nothing to say? Goddammit. You
             ungrateful—

HELEN   Where did these come from? Say something.

GEORGE   There is nothing to say. You squandered that
             money on toys, didn't you?

> CAMPBELL *looks at* MARK.

GEORGE	He's not going to help you. Look at me when I'm speaking to you!
	CAMPBELL turns to MATTHEW.
	He's not going to help you either. Will you look at me.
	CAMPBELL looks down.
	You even look guilty. Where is the rest of the money? You couldn't have spent it all.
	CAMPBELL looks at MARK again.
	Hey, hey, do you two know anything about this? If you do—
MATTHEW	No, sir.
MARK	No, sir.
GEORGE	Well? Where's the rest of it? Goddammit, boy! We give you food, shelter, an education— Get your clothes on—
HELEN	What? Where are you taking him?
GEORGE	To the station. *Now*, boy!
	GEORGE drags CAMPBELL off to the police station. HELEN follows.
MARK	Why didn't you say anything?
MATTHEW	Why didn't you...? I can still catch the ship....
MARK	But what about Campbell?
MATTHEW	Nine a.m. You promised.
MARK	You can't go now.
MATTHEW	No good-byes.

	MATTHEW *puts his letter on the table and exits.* MARK *is alone on stage. He paces. He sits. He stands and paces some more. He goes to his room and gets out his shipping notebook.*
MARK	*Inca Maru... Japan Maru... Nippon Maru... Pacific Maru.*
	The clock chimes and MARK *reacts. Rapidly:*
	Seven o'clock. *Pacific Maru*, registration Panama, built 1956, commissioned 1957, twelve thousand tons, three holds, industrial derricks for and aft, coal-fueled steam engines with maximum twenty knots, carries twelve passengers, bound for San Francisco, weighing anchor at 6:31 a.m. ....
	MARK *closes the book. He paces. He sits and hugs his knees. He gets up. He closes his eyes. The clock chimes.*
	Eight o'clock. Hurry up, hurry up.... *Pacific Maru*, registration Panama, built 1956, commissioned 1957.... *(etc)*
	MARK *repeats the specifications rapidly, like a mantra, underscoring the following.* GEORGE *and* HELEN *enter.*
GEORGE	He'll be in front of that magistrate in a few minutes.
	In a separate area, CAMPBELL *is pushed into a cone of light. He is in handcuffs.*
CAMPBELL	I do not recognize this court.
HELEN	We should have stayed.
GEORGE	He is no longer our responsibility.
	MARK *enters.*

MARK   What time is it?

HELEN   Mark.

GEORGE   Why aren't you in school?

> GEORGE *sees the letter, picks it up, and starts reading it.*

HELEN   Are you ill?

CAMPBELL   Say what you like.

> *In a separate area,* MATTHEW *is thrown into a cargo hold. He kneels.*

HELEN   Do you have a temperature?

MATTHEW   Dear God....

CAMPBELL   Not guilty! I did not steal the money!

MATTHEW   If you get me off this ship, I promise you—

MARK   What time is it?

HELEN   Just before nine.

MARK   What before nine?

HELEN   Two minutes to.

MATTHEW   Anything you want.

HELEN   You look a little pale.

CAMPBELL   I found the toys—

MATTHEW   I confess stealing the money—there!

HELEN   Open up.

MARK   Aaah.

MATTHEW	But, I don't deserve this cargo hold.
GEORGE	Helen.
HELEN	Looks fine.
GEORGE	Helen. Read this.
HELEN	What is it?
CAMPBELL	False accusations!
MATTHEW	I'm sorry.
MARK	What time is it?
GEORGE	*(to* MARK*)* Do you know anything about this?
MARK	What time is it?
GEORGE	Nine. Do you—
MARK	Exactly nine?
GEORGE	One minute to. Mark—
MATTHEW	Tell me what to do.
GEORGE	What the hell are you mumbling?
HELEN	Oh, God!
GEORGE	Do you know where Matthew is?
MARK	NO!
CAMPBELL	What? Me? Guilty?
MATTHEW	The police will arrest me at the next port.
CAMPBELL	How? Why?
GEORGE	What does this mean—?

He hands MARK *the letter.*

HELEN   "I will send for Mark when I am situated...."

CAMPBELL   Yes, I know who stole the money.

GEORGE   I'm waiting—

                    CAMPBELL *and* MARK *together:*

CAMPBELL   NO!

MARK   NO!

CAMPBELL   I will not tell.

MARK   Matthew—

MATTHEW   Yes?

GEORGE   Yes?

MATTHEW   So, I must escape.

HELEN   Please, where is he—?

MARK   I—

MATTHEW   But how?

MARK   I can't—

CAMPBELL   Guilty? Only because it's convenient for you!

GEORGE   Alright, then.

                    GEORGE *exits to fetch the cane.*

HELEN   Mark. Look at me—

CAMPBELL   I reject your court—

                    GEORGE *returns with the cane.*

GEORGE	Well?
HELEN	Wait
MATTHEW	Wait.
MATTHEW	For nightfall—
CAMPBELL	I reject your sentence—
HELEN	Mark, your brother may be in danger—
CAMPBELL	I reject your caning—
MATTHEW	And make a run for it.
GEORGE	Don't play the innocent.

> GEORGE *swishes the air with the cane.*
> CAMPBELL *reacts as though struck by the cane.*

HELEN	Say something.
GEORGE	Come on, come on—
MATTHEW	But—

> GEORGE *swishes the air with the cane.*
> CAMPBELL *winces in pain.*

CAMPBELL	Ha!
HELEN	Mark, please?
MARK	What time is it now?
GEORGE	This is bloody nonsense.

> *Another swish of the cane.* CAMPBELL
> *winces.*

CAMPBELL	Ha!

MATTHEW	Whatever you do—
HELEN	Do you remember him saying anything?
MATTHEW	Say nothing.

> *Another swish of the cane.* CAMPBELL *winces.*

CAMPBELL	Ha!
HELEN	Please, he's getting impatient with you—
MATTHEW	Rest now.
CAMPBELL	Students of the world unite!

> *Another swish.* CAMPBELL *winces.*

Defeat the British aggressors and all their running dogs!

GEORGE	One—

> *Another swish.* CAMPBELL *reacts.*

CAMPBELL	Dare to fight!
GEORGE	Two.
CAMPBELL	Defy difficulties!
GEORGE	That's it! Come here!
HELEN	No!

> GEORGE *thrashes the table three times with the cane.* CAMPBELL *reacts each time.* HELEN *covers her ears.*

CAMPBELL	I reject your punishment!

> HELEN *pulls* GEORGE *offstage.*

MATTHEW	Sleep.
CAMPBELL	I reject your pain!

CAMPBELL falls to his knees.

MATTHEW	Dream.

The clock chimes. MATTHEW *looks up.*

CAMPBELL	I will destroy you!
MARK	*PACIFIC MARU!*

The boys stare at each other.

Curtain.

End of Act I.

Act Two

> *It is one week later. In the dark, we hear chanting from demonstrators in the streets. The lights come up in the SIMMONS apartment. MARK is standing at the front windows of the apartment. He is looking at the demonstrators through his binoculars. HELEN and GEORGE are seated at the table, looking towards CAMPBELL's room. A paper-bag bomb explodes offstage. GEORGE and HELEN react.*

HELEN   Mark, come away from the balcony.

MARK   I will, in a sec.

GEORGE   *(stands, warning)* Mark—

HELEN   George, don't.

> *HELEN crosses to MARK and taps him on the shoulder. She gestures that she wants MARK inside. MARK complies. HELEN closes the French doors, locking out the sound of the demonstrators.*

That's better. Can't hear yourself think for all the shouting.

> *CAMPBELL enters from his room, carrying a cheap bag. He is holding his employment release form. HELEN looks at GEORGE, who nods.*

Gum-Bo... neigh sick jor fahn mah? [Campbell... have you had lunch yet?]

CAMPBELL	*Sick jor, ye-ow sum.* [Yes, thank you for asking.]
HELEN	I'll fix you something.
CAMPBELL	No. Thank you.
HELEN	It's no trouble—
CAMPBELL	I need this signed. It's my employment release.
HELEN	Yes.

> CAMPBELL *puts a piece of paper on the table.* HELEN *takes it.*

CAMPBELL	It must be signed by the head of the household....

> *Pause.*

Ah, yes, you want to inspect the contents of my bag. To ensure that nothing has been stolen.

> CAMPBELL *places his bag on the table.*

HELEN	That won't be necessary.
CAMPBELL	Then...?

> HELEN *looks at* GEORGE.

GEORGE	You see, the thing of it is this—
CAMPBELL	*Neigh m-sei tong ngaw gong.* [Don't talk to me.]
GEORGE	Now, just a minute—
HELEN	George... Campbell....

> CAMPBELL *grabs his bag off the table.*

HELEN   Campbell... there is something important I have to
               tell you. But before I do, I want you to know how
               sorry I am about what happened last week.... It was
               a terrible mistake.... I'm... we're *all* very sorry for
               what happened. Your place is here with us.

GEORGE   You see, the thing of it is... there is no necessity
               for you to go.... I understand how you must feel—

CAMPBELL   You understand nothing.

GEORGE   Now, just a minute. The whole money thing was a
               mistake, granted. And you heard my wife say how
               we all feel about it. But you were also going to be
               charged for stealing the toys. You don't know this,
               but I made sure those charges were dropped, because
               I spoke to the right people, returned those things,
               and so on. Now, what do you have to say about
               that?

CAMPBELL   My paper.

               GEORGE *and* CAMPBELL *glare at each
               other.* GEORGE *breaks from the stare,
               takes the paper from* HELEN *and signs it.*
               CAMPBELL *signals to* MARK *secretly,
               to meet him on the roof.*

HELEN   Wait.

GEORGE   Helen, it's what he wants. There, don't say I didn't
               want things to return to the status quo. I'm willing
               to overlook your role in stealing those toys. Put it
               behind us. Move forward—

               CAMPBELL *takes the employment
               release form from* GEORGE, *and exits.*

HELEN   Campbell, please, a few moments of your time.
               George, we agreed we would both apologize.

GEORGE	What do you want me to do now? Run after him?

MARK *is about to follow* CAMPBELL *out.*

GEORGE   Mark! Let him go.

MARK *stays.*

GEORGE   It's better this way. He's a resourceful fella. He'll be alright.... You see, Mark, he doesn't understand yet that—

HELEN   I wanted everyone together when—

GEORGE   No, now wait, I was not about to say anything.... As I was saying... he doesn't understand yet that we all have to compromise, make sacrifices.... See, when I was your age, no younger than you, my grandmother used to take me to the park, in Shanghai, to play on the swings. There was a sign at the entrance to the park which read: "No Dogs or Chinese Allowed." Grandmother had to wait outside, with the Chinese servants. But I was allowed in because I look.... She knew what sacrifice she had to make so that I would be accepted, even then I knew why she had to make that choice.

In life, we have to understand our differences, we have to make compromises, we have to make decisions and live by them.... You'll understand when you are older. It's better this way....

HELEN   Mark: *Yut ga yun tung toi sik fahn, yut ding yue fan gum tong mei.* Do you understand?

MARK   Something about eating from the same plate?

HELEN   Yes: "To be a family we must endeavour to eat from the same plate, so that we can always taste the same thing." You won't leave me too, will you?

> MARK *starts to leave.*

HELEN   Where are you going?

MARK   To the roof.

GEORGE   Just the roof. No going out into the street.

> MARK *exits.*

I have to get to the station. Martial law begins at sunset. There'll be riots any day now.

> CAMPBELL *appears on the roof with his bag.*

Best to pack a few things.

HELEN   Pack.

GEORGE   Just in case. Get as much canned food as you can. All businesses and schools are closed. The army will patrol the streets, and after dark they'll shoot first and ask questions later. Don't go out. Keep Mark at home.

> HELEN *sits down.* MARK *arrives on the roof.*

I'll call you from the station.

> GEORGE *exits.* CAMPBELL *is staring out towards where the demonstrators were.*

CAMPBELL   The still air signals a wild storm.

MARK   Yes, it's quiet.

> *He stands beside* CAMPBELL *and looks through his binoculars.*

MARK   They're gone.

CAMPBELL   Not gone... waiting. You ever see a cat before it
                leaps? It goes very still, pulls back all its muscles,
                concentrates, waits for the mouse to get confident,
                waits, then *(claps his hands)* BAM !

MARK   Aah!

                CAMPBELL *pokes* MARK *in the ribs,
                on the head, on his arm, etc.*

CAMPBELL   Got to be ready!

MARK   Stop that!

CAMPBELL   You aren't ready!

MARK   Quit it! Or—

CAMPBELL   Or what?

                CAMPBELL *stops poking.*

                Or nothing.... Why didn't you tell about the
                money?

MARK   You could have said something, too.

CAMPBELL   *M'ung ah!* [Idiot!]. I am Chinese, from the lower
                classes, a houseboy. We can't be trusted, we lie,
                we cheat, we steal all the time from our masters—
                don't you know that? Guilty until proven innocent.

                A moment.

MARK   He was my brother.

                A moment.

                Don't leave. Everybody always wants to leave. You
                could stay. It'll be different.

CAMPBELL   The *two* musketeers?

MARK   Will you still be my friend?

CAMPBELL   Friends...? Comrades! You look, but you do not
             see.

                     CAMPBELL *takes out a cigarette and*
                     lights it with his cigarette lighter.

             What you— What *we* experienced was oppression.

MARK   Oppression.

CAMPBELL   Yes. I didn't see it at first either. But the inmates
             told me at the infirmary. After lights out, every
             night the other prisoners gathered at the bed of this
             man. He gave me this. *(shows* MARK *the cigarette*
             lighter) And this. *(takes out a watch)*

MARK   Wow. Seiko.

CAMPBELL   And he told us these stories. About real heroes—
             not Batman or Superman—but real people, Chinese
             heroes, in China, who did these things.

MARK   What things?

CAMPBELL   Have you heard of the Long March?

MARK   No.

CAMPBELL   In the old days in China, farmers had to give all
             their food to the local warlord, who owned all the
             farms. So the farmers had nothing left for
             themselves or their families. But the warlords didn't
             care, and ordered the farmers to produce even more
             food, year after year.

MARK   That's not fair.

CAMPBELL   Right. So there was this group of farmers from this
             one place who got together, secretly, to find a way
             to kill their warlord. But the farmers had no guns or
             anything, and the warlord had the best weapons.

MARK   What kind?

CAMPBELL   Um... M-16s.

MARK   They didn't have M-16s in the old days.

CAMPBELL .   Well, maybe they were Lee-Enfields, I don't know.

MARK   Lugers. I bet the warlord carried a Luger side-arm.

CAMPBELL   Do you want to hear this story or not?

> *He takes the cigarette lighter from*
> MARK.

MARK   Yes, yes, so the farmers didn't have any guns....

CAMPBELL   Right, and not only that, they were outnumbered
                by warlords who had armies with jeeps and tanks
                and—

MARK   Artillery—

CAMPBELL   Yes, artillery. Now, the leader of this secret group
                of farmers decided to find out if there were other
                farmers who were treated as badly as the ones in his
                village. So he went to visit neighbouring
                provinces.

MARK   How did he get there?

CAMPBELL   He had a cart with a donkey. He travelled for almost
                a year and discovered that all the farmers in the
                whole country worked for warlords and never had
                money or food.

MARK   So, how did he travel for a year without food?

CAMPBELL   He killed the donkey and ate it, alright? Now, so,
                when he got back to his own village, he met
                secretly with his group and told them all the things
                he saw. When the warlords heard this, they prepared
                their armies to attack the helpless group of farmers.
                But Mao, who was very clever, saw the troops
                gathering, and—

MARK   Mao? You mean Mao-tze Tung?

CAMPBELL   Yes, he was the leader of this secret group of
               farmers. He got his group together, and one night
               they walked out of the village and into the hills.
               Farmers from across the country left their villages
               and joined him. When the warlords attacked the
               villages, there was nobody there. Then Mao and his
               followers went on this Long March deep into the
               interior of China. It took them three years to get far
               enough away from the pursuing armies of the
               warlords. Like Moses and the Israelites fleeing from
               Pharaoh and his army in "The Ten
               Commandments."

               Just imagine, marching until your shoes fall apart.
               Then you wrap your feet with cloth, which you tear
               from your clothes. And when you get hungry, you
               chew the bark of trees, and when you are thirsty,
               you melt snow in your hands.

               Many died and lost their families, but they found a
               new family in each other. No one owned anything.
               They shared all their belongings with their new
               community. They stayed together, they helped each
               other, supported each other. They remained loyal
               and walked over six thousand miles. Do you know
               how far that is?

MARK   No.

CAMPBELL   Well, it's very far.

MARK   But Mao, he's head of the Communists.

CAMPBELL   Yes, what's wrong with that?

MARK   He's a Communist.

CAMPBELL   So was Jesus.

                              Pause.

MARK   Was not.

CAMPBELL   Was too. Look, wasn't Jesus's homeland occupied
                by Roman warlords? And didn't the Romans own
                everything? Didn't Jesus and his people have to pay
                taxes to the Romans? Just like the farmers! And
                Jesus was the leader of a secret group of poor
                fishermen and they were persecuted just like the
                farmers. And whenever they got together they
                shared everything—food, drink. And they had to go
                into hiding too, and they formed a new community.
                Com-mu-nists.

MARK   Yeah, but Jesus was different.

CAMPBELL   You are right. The difference is that Mao survived.

                        Sound of helicopters in the distance.
                        MARK *looks through the binoculars.*

MARK   Helicopters. Army helicopters.

CAMPBELL   Let me see.

                        *He takes the binoculars. From the street
                        below, loud hailers blare out warnings.*

VOICE   Warning: Curfew will begin at eight p.m. Please
                stay off the street. Please stay off the street. Curfew
                will begin at eight p.m. Please stay off the
                street.... *(etc)*

                        *This is repeated in Cantonese as the jeep
                        drives past below. The helicopter comes
                        closer and closer.*

MARK   Here they come. *(referring to the helicopters)* Wow!

CAMPBELL   He said this would happen. Big storm coming.

MARK   They're heading for the Governor's house.

CAMPBELL   Yes.

                        *In the street, the sound of a truck
                        stopping, soldiers getting out.*

MARK   Look.

CAMPBELL   They've called out the army.

MARK   Wow.

CAMPBELL   Stay back, they'll see us. It's started.

MARK   What?

CAMPBELL   Running dogs! They are paper tigers. Look how scared they are. Warlords with helicopters, soldiers, guns—and we have only this.

> CAMPBELL *takes out his Little Red Book containing the sayings of Mao-tze Tung. A cone of light comes up on* GEORGE *in a separate area. He appears to be waiting for someone.*

The key, the answer to everything we are fighting for! Come!

MARK   Where?

CAMPBELL   I want you to meet my new comrades.

HELEN   *(from below)* Mark!

> *They freeze.*

CAMPBELL   Come, it's a secret meeting.

HELEN   Mark, can you hear me?!

CAMPBELL   All for one....

> CAMPBELL *holds his Little Red Book up in the air, like a sword.* MARK *thinks for a moment. Then he stretches his arm up and grasps the book.*

BOTH   And one for all!

CAMPBELL   Keep your head down.

> *The boys exit.* HELEN *appears on the roof.*

HELEN   Mark!

> *She sees that* MARK *has gone.*

HELEN   Oh, Mark!

> CHIEF SUPERINTENDENT STERLING *enters. He stands in the shadow, outside the cone of light illuminating* GEORGE. *Helicopter and loudspeaker sounds end.*

STERLING   Ah, Simmons, waiting long?

GEORGE   No, sir.

STERLING   George, right?

GEORGE   Right, sir.

> HELEN *has returned downstairs. She sits and listens to the following.*

STERLING   How's the wife?

GEORGE   Very well, thank you.

STERLING   Two boys, if memory serves.

GEORGE   That's right, sir.

STERLING   KG Five School ?

GEORGE   Eh, no sir....

STERLING   Ah, I forgot, Catholic. So it's the other one. On the island? Expensive?

GEORGE   Yes.

STERLING   Hmmm?

GEORGE   Sir.

STERLING   Any news on... Matthew, is it?

GEORGE   No, sir... nothing.

STERLING   Must be difficult.

GEORGE   We manage, sir.

STERLING   Yes, we all slave to give our children what we never had. Sometimes wonder if the little buggers appreciate it.

GEORGE   Was there something you wished to discuss, sir?

STERLING   Yes, how are things down in the bowels of the building?

GEORGE   In the forty-eight hours since martial law, there have been increasing runs on the banks. The commies are very organized. They have leaders, men and women, who spread rumours and withdraw large sums of money, which rapidly turns into a panic among other depositors.... It's all in the report.

STERLING   Yes, but what do *you* think?

GEORGE   Me?

STERLING   Personally.

GEORGE   Well, I....

STERLING   Packing your suitcases, just in case? Getting your passport ready, perhaps?

GEORGE   It'll blow over. It did in '57.

STERLING   You think so. The demonstrations and protests are even more frequent this week.

GEORGE   They are mainly teenagers—a swift kick up the arse from the emergency squad—

STERLING   You employed a boy named Campbell Wong?

GEORGE   Yes....

STERLING   He was charged with theft....

GEORGE   Yes....

STERLING   Found guilty and caned.

GEORGE   He is no longer in our employ.

STERLING   And rightly so.

GEORGE   Is there something—

STERLING   And your boy Mark.

GEORGE   Yes... Mark.... Look, sir, it was a prank, just a boy's prank, I've returned the toys to the shop... the charges were dropped—

STERLING   Whatever are you talking about?

GEORGE   Well, they were caught shoplifting—

STERLING   Shoplifting?

GEORGE   Dinky Toys.

STERLING   Ha! I used to do that myself. Just means he'll grow up to be a Chief Superintendent one day, that's all. No, no, I don't know anything about that, no, no.... Here, have a look at these.

              STERLING *gives* GEORGE *a file folder.*
              GEORGE *opens it. He reads the single-sheet report, looks at photographs.*

GEORGE   Impossible.

STERLING   Photographs.

GEORGE   There must be some mistake. I would have known.... Where...?

STERLING   One of our operatives. It was taken at a Red Guard meeting in Kowloon Tong area. They study the works of Chairman Mao, get the kids all stirred up—

GEORGE   I'll put a stop to it immediately—

> GEORGE *begins to leave.*

STERLING   I would prefer you didn't.

GEORGE   Eh?

STERLING   He could be useful....

GEORGE   Useful.

STERLING   A source....

> *Pause.*

GEORGE   A source?

STERLING   An informant, that sort of thing.... Her Majesty's Government will be grateful....

GEORGE   But, he's my son....

STERLING   Very grateful.

GEORGE   It's too dangerous. And what if the situation escalates—?

STERLING   Escalates—American word.

GEORGE   Gets worse, worsens. In the last two days alone, the random bombings—

STERLING   But, as you say, a swift kick up the arse....

GEORGE   Yes, but this is—

STERLING   Different.... Look, this is all a bit of a shock....
                How about a pint, upstairs...? George...?

GEORGE   Huh...? Um....

STERLING   A short one? Upstairs?

GEORGE   I'm on duty, sir.

STERLING   John....

GEORGE   John.

STERLING   Time we got to know each other. Where're you
                from?

GEORGE   Um... my people come from Dunfree.

STERLING   Dunfree, Dunfree... ah! Dumfries *(pronounced
                "Dumfreeze")*

GEORGE   Dumfries! Yes, that's right.

STERLING   Coming?

GEORGE   Yes, thank you, sir.

STERLING   John.

GEORGE   John.

STERLING   Mark's our man, isn't he?

                        STERLING *exits with the file folder.*
                        MARK *enters on the roof. He is reading
                        from the Little Red Book. He checks the
                        time periodically, on his wrist watch.*

HELEN   But how can Mark possibly be "useful"... a
                "source"....? An "informant" did he say?

GEORGE   Ssssh! Where is he?

HELEN   In his room... on the roof....

GEORGE   He wants names, places... when they will strike, anything, everything.

HELEN   You didn't agree... did you...? George?

GEORGE   But we'll get passports... he promised real passports... with the right of abode.... I only need to monitor his movements. We must maintain the upper hand and crush this, this uprising. We must make a stand now and show those commies who's boss—

HELEN   George—

GEORGE   They won't get away with it this time.

HELEN   No.

GEORGE   Mark can't get very far, and he has to return before dark, before the curfew—

HELEN   They jump roofs. He's up there one minute and when I try to find him, he's gone. He doesn't have to use the streets.

GEORGE   But he always returns.

HELEN   Yes, he always comes home.

GEORGE   He's a good boy.

HELEN   He's all the children I have left.

                    GEORGE *and* HELEN *attempt to hold each other.*

                    MARK *reads from the Little Red Book:*

MARK	"In China, although the main socialist transformation has been completed with respect to the system of ownership, and although the large-scale and turbulent class-struggles of the proletariat masses, characteristic of the previous revolutionary periods have, in the main, come to an end, there are still remnants of the overthrown landlord...."

> MARK *checks his watch, then quickly lifts his binoculars and looks through them. There is a "thump" in the distance.* GEORGE *and* HELEN *look out as well. Sirens blare, heading towards the "thump" sound.*

GEORGE There's another one.

HELEN Paper-bag bomb.

GEORGE Sounded like it. *(calling towards* MARK*'s room)* Mark?

> MARK *checks his watch.*

MARK Five, four, three—

> MARK *swings his binoculars in a different direction. There is another "thump." Sirens blare toward the explosion.*

HELEN He must be up on the roof.

GEORGE Make sure he doesn't go anywhere.

> GEORGE *exits.* HELEN *exits to pack.* MARK *lowers his binoculars and returns to the Little Red Book. Unseen by* MARK, SARAH *appears and tiptoes up to him.*

MARK   "Although the main socialist transformation has
                been completed with respect to the system of
                ownership... system of ownership... main socialist
                transformation... *proletariat* masses... there are still
                remnants of the overthrown landlord... land-lord...
                war-lord....

SARAH   Boo!

                        MARK *hides the book behind his back.*
                        He puts it in his back pocket at an
                        appropriate moment during the following.

                What you reading?

MARK   Nothing.

SARAH   Hi.

MARK   Sarah....

SARAH   The one and only.

                        MARK *looks to see if anyone is coming.*

MARK   Sarah....

SARAH   Mark.... Sarah, Mark. Mark, Sarah.

MARK   How did you get up here?

SARAH   I'm not stupid. I only needs to be shown once....

MARK   No, I mean, the soldiers in the street—

SARAH   Oh, them, they all know me—even got an armed
                escort to your back stairs.

                        She looks over the edge of the roof and
                        waves.

SARAH   Can't stay long though. 'Ere, why haven't you
                called me back? It's been over a week.

Pause.

MARK   Um....

SARAH   I left so many messages for you.... Then I thought, well, if the mountain won't come to me, then I must go to the mountain.... Cat got your tongue? You must admit it was pretty embarrassing to be dancing in the caff with your boyfriend one minute, and then "poof" he's gone the next.

MARK   Oh, that.

SARAH   Yes, that. Jane said I should forget about you, but I thought, no, I'll give you another chance. So....

MARK   So....

He checks his watch.

Perhaps I can call you later.

SARAH   Oh no, you don't. I want an explanation now.

MARK   Explanation?

SARAH   I'm not leaving until I get one... or at least an apology....

MARK   I'm sorry.

SARAH   You're forgiven. Now, you won't do it again will you?

MARK   No.

SARAH   Good.... Well, that's that, then.

MARK   Yes.

MARK *looks to see if anyone is coming. Then* MARK *and* SARAH *speak at the same time:*

MARK   It's getting close to curfew, and you really
                shouldn't be away from—

SARAH   Right, well I thought, why not start at the
                beginning and forget—

BOTH   Sorry.

MARK   You first.

SARAH   OK.... Well... I rewrote that story and... I'm not
                going to enter it in the short-story contest
                because... well, it's too personal. It says how I
                feel, and I want to give it to you... it'll be our
                secret....

MARK   That's very thoughtful. I'm actually relieved.

SARAH   We're on stand-by to evacuate. I want you to have
                something to remember me by.... Here.

MARK   Thanks.

SARAH   I hope you like it.

MARK   I know I will.

SARAH   Now, what were you going to say?

MARK   I was going to say... to call... and ask you if we
                could, if you would like to....

                        CAMPBELL *enters, leaping onto the
                        roof.*

CAMPBELL   Did you see? Boom, right on time, I told you—

                        Pause. MARK *hides* SARAH's
                        manuscript behind his back.

SARAH   What's he doing here?

MARK   Campbell—

CAMPBELL	*Ng-or wah jor neigh tang. Ng-or sing Wong, gew Bei Tein.* [I told you. I am Wong, called Northern Heaven.]
SARAH	It's not dinner time, is it?
CAMPBELL	What's that? What are you hiding?
MARK	Nothing.

> CAMPBELL *lunges at* MARK *and manages to snatch the manuscript from him.*

CAMPBELL	Imperialist literature! *(tries to tear it)*
MARK	Don't!
SARAH	Hey!

> SARAH *lunges for the manuscript several times during the following. But each time,* CAMPBELL *manages to escape her.*

CAMPBELL	Poisonous sentiment!
SARAH	Give it back.
MARK	Campbell!
CAMPBELL	*Wong Bei Teen!* [Wong, Northern Heaven!]
SARAH	You have no right. What do you think you're doing—
CAMPBELL	La la la la la la—
SARAH	Give it back. Make him give it here.
MARK	*Bei Teen!* [Northern Heaven!]

> CAMPBELL *stops.*

| CAMPBELL | Yes? |

> *MARK holds his hand out for the manuscript.*

SARAH   I'll call the soldiers.

CAMPBELL   I'll burn it.

> *CAMPBELL takes out a cigarette lighter and flicks it on. The flame is under the manuscript.*

CAMPBELL   Ha! The tigress has no teeth. You see, made of paper.

> *CAMPBELL dips the manuscript into the flame.*

MARK   No!

SARAH   He's mad. He's a mad commie.

CAMPBELL   Mad? Missy die bahn wanna see little Chinee go mad? OK, missy.

> *CAMPBELL jumps about in a mocking, maniacal fashion. He sets the manuscript on fire.*

MARK   Stop it! Stop it!

> *MARK grabs the manuscript and stamps out the fire. The manuscript is charred but not destroyed. CAMPBELL stops jumping.*

SARAH   My story!

CAMPBELL   *Gie-eeu kui gee-ow la.* [Tell her to leave.]

SARAH   Speak English. Go away.

MARK   It's just charred.

CAMPBELL   You wan me speekee dee Ing-leash? Perhaps you would care for some tea? Won the quinella at the races t'other day, have to find a new *amah*, the last one robbed us blind—

SARAH   Let's go to my house. We can talk there.

CAMPBELL   You go. He stay.

SARAH   Stupid git.

CAMPBELL   Git? *You* co *me* git?

SARAH   Don't talk to me in that tone! I'll report you.

CAMPBELL·   Ha! No can do. No more houseboy.

SARAH   You're just a stupid little Chinee.

CAMPBELL   Oh, now I's stoo-peed.

> SARAH *takes* MARK's *hand.*

            When t'la-bo come, where she go? England. You fing she tik you wif her? Ha? Who's stoo-peed low?

SARAH   Mark, I don't like it here.

MARK   Campbell—

CAMPBELL   *Bei Tien!* [Northern Heaven!]

> MARK *starts to leave with* SARAH.
> CAMPBELL *blocks their way.*

CAMPBELL   He can't leave Hong Kong. No passport. He is stuck here like me, like all local people. Don't believe me? Ask him. Go on, ask him.

MARK   *Sau seng!* [I forbid you to say anything more!]

CAMPBELL   Ha! He is a local boy, born here, not from England. He is half Chinee, another stupid little Chinee like me.

MARK   How dare you—

SARAH   You're raving—

CAMPBELL   *M'ho cho.* [Shuttup.]

SARAH   Speak English!

CAMPBELL   Shuttup!

SARAH   You shuttup!

MARK   Everybody shut up!

Pause. MARK *leaves with* SARAH.

CAMPBELL   *Kui jo mutt yeh bay neigh ah? Kui duck ling neigh gor dye gor fahn lay mah? Gnor duck ah!* [What can she do for you? Can she bring your brother home? I can!]

MARK   What?

CAMPBELL   *Neigh geh dye gor fahn jor lay ah!* [Your brother has returned!]

SARAH   What's he saying?

CAMPBELL   Soo is lot for you. Running Dog. Paper Tiger. Do not care about little colonial boys like you or me.

SARAH   Right. Coming?

CAMPBELL   He's back. *Hi ya! Gnor m'hi neigh chair dye bow ah.* [Yes sirree! I wouldn't bullshit you.]

MARK   *Kui hi been seuw ah!* [Where is he?]

SARAH   What's going on? Who's back?

CAMPBELL   *Gew kui giow lah.* [Tell her to leave.]

SARAH   Mark?

MARK   *(to* CAMPBELL*)* I don't believe you.

SARAH   Believe what?

CAMPBELL   *Neigh tung gnor lay-ah, neigh gee geh tie lah mah.*
                [You come with me, you can see for yourself.]

MARK   *Chair dye bow!* [Bullshit!]

CAMPBELL   *Neigh tung gn'or lay-lah. Kui tongue neigh ah!*
                [Then come with me. He is waiting for you!]

SARAH   Mark, for the last time, are you coming?

                        A long pause.

                Are you coming?

MARK   No.

CAMPBELL   Ha!

SARAH   But—

MARK   Here. I don't want it....

                        MARK *holds the manuscript out.*

                Go away.

SARAH   What?

MARK   Go away....

                        MARK *thrusts the charred manuscript into*
                        SARAH's *hands.*

                Leave—you said you wanted to. I don't want to see
                you again....

SARAH	You can't mean that....
MARK	And besides, you're not a very good writer....
SARAH	Mark.

> CAMPBELL *waves his hand dismissively at* SARAH.

CAMPBELL	Go!
SARAH	What did you say to him? What did he say to you?
CAMPBELL	*Giow lah!* [Let's go.]

> CAMPBELL *exits.* MARK *looks at* SARAH, *then exits.* SARAH *is alone. In the street, military jeeps drive by slowly. Loud hailers blare:*

VOICE   Warning! Please stay off the street. Remain in your homes. Warning! Please stay off the street. Remain in your homes.

> *The message is repeated in Cantonese.*

> SARAH *exits. As the boys jump from roof to roof, evening approaches and police warnings compete with demonstrators' chanting. Overhead, army helicopters are on patrol. Slides show crowds in the streets.*

> *On a different roof,* CAMPBELL *leaps onstage. He extends his hands towards* MARK, *who is offstage.*

CAMPBELL	Come on, jump.
MARK	*(off)* How many more?
CAMPBELL	Jump!

> MARK *leaps onstage.*

CAMPBELL   Did you finish the book I gave you?

               MARK *checks behind him.*

               "The Thoughts of Chairman Mao"?

MARK   This way?

                         MARK *exits, followed by* CAMPBELL.
                         When they are offstage, MATTHEW
                         appears. He exits in the direction of the
                         other boys. The police warnings continue
                         to compete with the chanting of
                         demonstrators. Overhead, army helicopters
                         are on patrol. Slides show crowds in the
                         streets.

                         On yet another roof, MATTHEW *leaps*
                         onstage. He talks to the others, who are
                         offstage.

MATTHEW   Further back. OK, now!

                         CAMPBELL *and* MARK *leap onstage*
                         simultaneously.

               Good one. Watch this!

                         MATTHEW *and* CAMPBELL *start to*
                         leave.

MARK   Matthew!

MATTHEW   What?

MARK   Where are you taking me? When did you get back?

MATTHEW   Not here. C'mon.

                         MATTHEW *grabs* MARK, *and together*
                         with CAMPBELL, *they exit. The boys*
                         enter on another roof, far from home.

MATTHEW   'Owzat?

MARK	Wow! That was at least ten feet across.
MATTHEW	Ten, eight and three quarters, to be exact.
CAMPBELL	Able to leap tall buildings in a single bound! Super brothers!
MARK	I jumped all the way from home.
MATTHEW	Told you you could do it one day.
MARK	Yeah, wow! Where is the widest?
MATTHEW	Over there! Three buildings over. Twelve and a half feet! I'll get it one day.
CAMPBELL	We can talk here.

They sit as though around a campfire.

MATTHEW	Right. The patrols haven't moved in this direction yet.
CAMPBELL	*(to MARK)* See what I told you? Together again. The three harmonies: Heaven, Earth, Man.
MATTHEW	Brutus, Cassius, Casca.
CAMPBELL	Revolutionaries against Caesar—oppressor of the people.
MATTHEW	Anarchists!
MARK	I thought you said you were going to America.
MATTHEW	I tried. I was on that ship for three days. The Master got cold feet, the bastard, and he put me on a trawler headed back here.
MARK	Mum and Dad were worried sick.
MATTHEW	Dad give it to you?
MARK	No— I mean, yeah— but I didn't tell.

MATTHEW	I knew you wouldn't.... Seven days in a cargo hold, first on that freighter... a rust bucket with rats the size of Chihuahuas... then stuck in a corner of the trawler for another three days, fish on one side, me on the other... another couple of days hungry, hiding, looking for him.
CAMPBELL	Now he owe me again!
MARK	You've joined the Red Guards?
MATTHEW	No, it's not like that. It's... something else... something in here.... Red Guards, Father screaming at me, Mother making excuses, all of it—
MARK	Never mind, we'll make it better at home.
CAMPBELL	Huh!
MATTHEW	Home. What's that?
CAMPBELL	There is no more "home."
MATTHEW	Things have changed, Mark.... See, I've always done what they wanted... that is, everything *he* wanted.... Cricket—
MARK	First eleven!
MATTHEW	The youngest member of the Club team. Tennis—
MARK	You said you'd show me the googlie—
MATTHEW	And he watched me, watched me like a hawk.
MARK	He was proud of you.
MATTHEW	Proud of me? No, no.... Oh, he cheered alright, when I hit a "four" or a "six." All that was fine... "third man" on the team... but after the match, I was just a boy sitting outside the clubhouse bar.

MATTHEW   Usually, I'd get on my bike and ride home. But, this one time, I had to wait for him. "Drinks all 'round," he said. A cheer. A toast to the Queen and they were all transported, magically, to an English village pub—singing songs, telling bad jokes, and talking about the sea-side in July. He was right at home with them, though he had never set foot in England in his life—everything he knew, he learned from British films, from books and records at the Council library.... His accent he got from the BBC overseas service.... And they believed him....

More drinks. More stories. Nodding, smiling as wide as his face could hold. Face red with alcohol and heat, eyes gleaming with pride that he was accepted as one of them. More drinks. More stories... on and on.... Then... the laughing stopped. The songs stopped. I looked in....

The bar was littered with half-eaten scotch eggs, empty glasses, spilled beer. In the silence, a faint panting from a line-up of men. Still and panting, exhausted from running away, suddenly sad to rediscover where they were. Here, not there. One of them said: "Trapped on a pimple growing on China's bottom, suffering from diarrhea, prickly heat, reading week-old newspapers, and counting the days...." Then, hatred popped out of their mouths, like mortar shells exploding around the Chinese bartenders: "Chink, wog, gook, Fu Manchu, commie, pinko, slopehead...." And you know what he said?

OTHERS   What?

MATTHEW   "Wontonners!" *He* called the bartenders "Wontonners."

CAMPBELL *spits.*

He was in there with the whole slobbering, sweaty bunch, calling the bartenders names, until the laughing started again.... That scene kept playing over and over in my head....

MARK	What did you expect him to do?
	MATTHEW *and* CAMPBELL *look at* MARK.
CAMPBELL	Blind!
MATTHEW	What did I expect? He's half-Chinese.
CAMPBELL	A blind boy!
MATTHEW	Don't you see? He was wrong to pretend.
CAMPBELL	*Hey yeow chee lay.* [Bloody hell.]
MARK	Compromise! The bartenders didn't say anything because they knew their place, they made a sacrifice so that Dad could—
CAMPBELL	Ai ya!
MATTHEW	Don't you see, he hates himself, hates who he is. And I'm afraid... I'm afraid if I stay, I'll become like him. I don't want to be afraid anymore. I must strike while the iron is hot!
CAMPBELL	Make the iron hot by striking!
MARK	Brutus and Cassius fell on their own swords.
MATTHEW	No more compromise!
CAMPBELL	No more sacrifice! Bartenders, coolies, factory workers, houseboy, all the same—proletariat. No more compromise. When I was your houseboy, you know where I lived? In a room smaller than your closet. Sacrifice.
MARK	At least you had a room of your own. I had to share mine!

A moment.

And what's a "proletariat" anyway?

CAMPBELL	What?

> MARK *takes out the Little Red Book and tosses it at* CAMPBELL.

MARK	In there. "Proletariat."
CAMPBELL	"Workers." Factory workers. Have you seen how *they* live?
MARK	Who?
CAMPBELL	The workers.

> CAMPBELL *grabs* MARK*'s head and spins him in various directions.*

CAMPBELL	Look—there. Those people in those shacks on the side of that hill. And on that one, and that one!
MARK	Let go!
MATTHEW	Easy.

> CAMPBELL *releases* MARK.

CAMPBELL	You had your say. My turn now. Huh? What about them?
MARK	I'm not allowed there. It's full of drug addicts and disease—
CAMPBELL	Shacks made of cardboard or... or sheets of metal.... No toilets, no running water, no refrigeration. And when the typhoons come, everything is destroyed, sluiced down the side of the hill. Then they get "resettled" in government apartment slums, flats— thirty-feet by ten-feet, children and parents sleep in the same room, bunk beds stacked three or four high, a stinking wood stove on the balcony mixing with the smoke and stench from factories across the street, old people working until they are eighty,

CAMPBELL	*(con't)* single men sleeping in cages the size of a single bed—like dogs in kennels, compared with the rich in big houses on the Peak, driving around in Rolls Royces. Sacrifice! Compromise! There will be blood in the *nullahs* before that happens to us again!

CAMPBELL *crouches, exhausted.*

MARK	What do you want... what am I supposed to do... I can't... I don't want to lose... I want... I want....
MATTHEW	Easy, easy.... *(to MARK)* How's Sarah?
MARK	OK....
MATTHEW	Good. That's good. Look, tomorrow night I want you to leave home. Meet me here and we'll run away together just like I said we would.
MARK	Why don't you come home? I won't let him hit you, it'll be different.
CAMPBELL	Confucius say: "Man who put head in sand leave buttocks in air to be kicked."
MATTHEW	I can't.
MARK	Why'd you have to run away? And why'd you go and have to get arrested? Why don't... you just... come home... both of you?
CAMPBELL	Ha!
MATTHEW	Tomorrow we're going to attack Government House.
MARK	We?
CAMPBELL	There will be hundreds of comrades, more than they expect. We'll break through the line, and charge up the hill with molotov cocktails!
MARK	Are you commies, then?

MATTHEW   I could give a shit about his revolution.

CAMPBELL   What did you say?

MATTHEW   I could care less if you're red, green, or purple. You
               need another bomb thrower, and I can't get close
               enough without you. I'm just doing what I have to
               do.

                         Helicopters close. MATTHEW *and*
                         CAMPBELL *stand.*

MARK   But why? What are you fighting for?

MATTHEW   Damn, they're sweeping this sector. Twelve and a
               half feet. You ready?

CAMPBELL   *Chee seen ah!* [He's mad!]

MATTHEW   You're chicken soup.

                         Helicopters closer. MATTHEW *and*
                         CAMPBELL *run to the left. Helicopters
                         closer.*

MATTHEW   Mark, come on.

CAMPBELL   *Geow lah, kui geen neigh ah.* [Let's go, they'll see
               you.]

                         MARK *does not move.* MATTHEW *and*
                         CAMPBELL *stretch out their hands
                         towards* MARK.

MATTHEW   Mark, we can't stay, you have to come now.

CAMPBELL   *Lei-ah, lei-ah.* [Come on, come on.]

MATTHEW   For God's sake, Mark!

CAMPBELL   *Lei-ah, lei-ah.* [Come on, come on.]

                         Helicopters almost overhead. MATTHEW
                         and CAMPBELL *exit left.*

MATTHEW	*(off)* Mark!
CAMPBELL	*(off) Geow lah, geow lah.* [Let's go, let's go.]

> MARK *stands up slowly. As the helicopter search lights paint the stage, we see* MARK *sprint in the opposite direction, away from* MATTHEW *and* CAMPBELL.
>
> *Helicopters roar overhead. Search lights wash over the empty roof tops. Gradually, the helicopters fade in the distance.*
>
> *A cone of light comes up on* GEORGE. *He is speaking to* STERLING, *who is offstage.*

GEORGE   Sir, the thing of it is... I won't do it... I will not ask Mark to... I will not risk the safety of my son....

> GEORGE *waits.*

Sir?

> STERLING *enters, wiping his hands on a towel.*

STERLING   I heard you.

GEORGE   Well, that's that, then.

STERLING   Yes.

GEORGE   About the passports—

STERLING   Well, of course, you can hardly expect Her Majesty's Government to be grateful for your response.... Serious, very serious.

GEORGE   There are far more reliable sources.

STERLING   I am very disappointed. Very disappointed.

GEORGE	These are kids, for heaven's sake—
STERLING	Hooligans with no respect for the law.
GEORGE	I do not see why—
STERLING	Are you questioning my motives?
GEORGE	There are regulations governing the employment of minors. There is no necessity in this case—
STERLING	I decide what is necessary in this department.... Coming up to what? Fifteen years on the force?
GEORGE	Sixteen, sir.
STERLING	And only an Inspector. Why do you think that is? You see, this was an opportunity for you.... It comes down to loyalty, doesn't it...? I mean, how do I know if I can rely on you from now on...? Where is your loyalty, George...? Is it with us?
GEORGE	That has never been in question.
STERLING	Until now.
GEORGE	Let me prove it.
STERLING	Well now, what can we do, what can we do.... Have a look at this.

> STERLING *gives* GEORGE *an order paper.*

STERLING	You will execute those orders.
GEORGE	Yes.
STERLING	Yes, what?
GEORGE	Yes, sir.

> STERLING *exits. The cone of light dissolves.*
>
> *Lights up on* SARAH, *who is on the roof of the* SIMMONS *apartment. She looks about, waiting. After a moment,* MARK *leaps onto the roof. Helicopters in the distance.*

SARAH   Mark! Oh, thank God it's you at last.

MARK   It's after curfew.

SARAH   I know.

MARK   Have you been here all this time?

SARAH   No....

> *Sound of knocking. Lights up on the* SIMMONS *apartment below.*

SARAH   Not here, exactly....

> HELEN *enters with a suitcase, which she places on the table, then crosses off to answer the front door.*

Well, sort of....

MARK   You should be at home.

HELEN   *(off)* You should be at home.

SARAH   It's terribly important. Oh, sod—I went to see your mother.

> SARAH *crosses into the apartment.* MARK *follows her.*

MARK   What did you go and do that for?

SARAH   I thought you were in danger.

HELEN	What do you mean?
SARAH	He's with that Campbell, your houseboy.
HELEN	You saw them together?
SARAH	*(to* HELEN*)* They leapt from building to building. I lost sight of them.
HELEN	Mark will come back.
SARAH	*(to* HELEN*)* Are you sure?
HELEN	Of all of them, I'm surest about him.
SARAH	*(to* MARK*)* I'm sorry.... *(to* HELEN*)* I'm not normally like this, but I care about Mark. *(to* MARK*)* I had to tell her.
MARK	What did she say?
HELEN	Do your parents know?
SARAH	No, not really.
HELEN	Good, that's good.
SARAH	Me da's on duty at the barracks, 'round the clock, and me mum's busy packing, in case—
HELEN	Yes, it's best to be prepared.
SARAH	I'm worried about Mark, Missuss.
HELEN	I know.
SARAH	So, I've come to see you, as one woman to another.... We've got to get him away from that commie. He's a bad influence. I just know he is. Chinese can't be trusted, they don't think like us, do they?
HELEN	I didn't give him your telephone messages.

SARAH   You didn't?

HELEN   No.

SARAH   Why not?

HELEN   We don't think Mark is old enough to have a girlfriend.

          HELEN *gets up and moves away from her seat.*

SARAH   Oh... I see.... And Campbell?

MARK   What about him?

SARAH   What are we going to do about him?

HELEN   Nothing.

MARK   Nothing.

SARAH   *(to* HELEN*)* Nothing? You won't let him have a girlfriend, but you will let him have a Chinee commie as a friend—

HELEN   Yes.

SARAH   Why?

HELEN   They belong together.

SARAH   Belong together? But he's mad, and he's turning Mark's mind—

HELEN   Campbell is my son. *(pause)* Aaah.... "My son." So good to say those words out loud.

SARAH   But he's a houseboy.

HELEN   Yes.

SARAH   I don't understand—why is he a houseboy if he is your son?

A moment.

HELEN   Let me ask you this. You care about Mark?

SARAH   Yes, very much.

HELEN   And how much are you willing to pay for him?

SARAH   "Pay"—you mean money? I don't have any money—

HELEN   "Pay." No, not the right word. Not money... you... in here... how much?

SARAH *does not understand.*

HELEN   Woman to woman... let me tell you one woman's story.... The communists took over Shanghai and my husband George went there to rescue his grandmother. He angered the communist authorities with his demands and they jailed him.... Silence... nothing... no news, no letters for one year, five months and eighteen days.... Seventeen months lost from my life... five hundred and thirty-three dreary days and nights of waiting and longing and praying.... Matthew was just a baby. He wouldn't remember.

I had an affair. The baby came... I didn't tell the father. Couldn't, anyway. He disappeared.... I gave him up for adoption. Did you know that when you give your baby up for adoption, they don't even let you see him or... hold him...? It was for the best....

George's grandmother died in a communist jail and they expelled George back to Hong Kong. They gave him back his life and a stack of letters he had written to me. They didn't mail them. I read them all in one night.... I decided not to tell him about the baby....

HELEN	Then Mark was born.... I held the boys... so tight... spoiled them. The thought of Campbell, abandoned in an orphanage, was too much.... I needed to be a mother to *all* my children, and so, I brought Campbell home.... I told George... he was very angry....

> GEORGE *enters in a separate area.*

Liar!

> GEORGE *slaps the air, then exits.*
> HELEN *cups the side of her face with the palm of one hand.*

HELEN	It hurt for days... but we worked it out. George remained loyal to me. To avoid a scandal, to keep up appearances, George became Campbell's godfather and we took him in... as a houseboy.... I am the fulcrum of a delicate balance. A small price to pay for having all my children together.

> HELEN *crosses to the suitcase and takes out a framed photo. She hands it to* SARAH, *who examines it studiously.*

SARAH	Who?
HELEN	My parents.

> HELEN *takes out a second framed picture.*

HELEN	George's grandmother.
SARAH	Chinee.
HELEN	I assure you we are very trustworthy people....
SARAH	What I said before... about Chinese people... I didn't mean you... I mean... I'm sorry... I don't know what I meant....

HELEN   I do.... In dramas, melodramas, the characters can
               take the easy way out—a vile of poison, a leap off
               some high cliff—but here, we have to make
               decisions about who we are every day, we have to
               decide which plate of the scale to tip without
               upsetting the balance. The stakes are high. You
               have to ask yourself: How much am I willing to
               give to this role? Am I up to it?

                              A beat.

HELEN   Do you want children?

SARAH   Children?

HELEN   Someday?

SARAH   Yes, someday... yes, I think I would....

HELEN   And when that time comes, you will want to do the
               very best you can for your children, too. Mark is...
               inside here, he is Chinese. He doesn't know it yet,
               but he will, one day. He should stay with his own.

SARAH   But—

HELEN   You see, no matter what happens out there, you—
               all of you—can leave. But we have to stay. This is
               our home. Can you understand that?

                              Pause.

SARAH   Yes.

HELEN   Good.

SARAH   Will you tell him—

                       HELEN *raises a finger to her own lips.*
                       Helicopter approach.

HELEN   It's for the best. Woman to woman.

> HELEN *touches* SARAH*'s cheek, then*
> *puts her arm around* SARAH*'s shoulder*
> *and leads her off.*
>
> *Helicopters closer.* HELEN *sits at the*
> *table and takes out her rosary.*

MARK	Oh, God.
SARAH	No, it's alright... it's alright.... I had to come and tell you that it doesn't change anything for me.
MARK	You don't understand.
SARAH	Yes, I do. You're part Chinese and it doesn't matter. That's what you tried to tell me before. You don't have to be ashamed of who you are, not with me, not anymore.
MARK	Oh God, Sarah.
SARAH	I've stayed far too long.... Mark...? When this is all over, I want to continue.... I don't know how, but we'll find a way... won't we...? Mark...? I have to go.... Please tell me it'll be alright.
MARK	They're going to bomb Government House.
SARAH	What?
MARK	Campbell and Matthew—tomorrow.
SARAH	What are you talking about?
MARK	They don't even know what they're doing.
SARAH	Mark, are they in danger? Your brothers? What do you mean "bomb Government House"?
MARK	What am I going to do?

SARAH   Do you mean they're.... Oh, my God... you have
          to do something.... I have to go, I have to go....
          Tell your da, get a message to them, something,
          they're family.... Oh fudge, fudge, fudge. Mark,
          promise me you'll do something!

              *SARAH exits. Helicopters roar overhead.
              MARK screams, but he is drowned out by
              the sound of the helicopters. MARK exits.*

VOICE   Warning: Curfew. Please stay off the street. Please
          stay off the street. Curfew. Please stay off the
          street.

              The message is repeated in Cantonese.

              *The next day. Lights come up in the
              SIMMONS apartment. MARK is looking
              through his binoculars. HELEN enters.*

HELEN   Here we are. Nice hot cuppa cha. George!

              GEORGE enters.

GEORGE   Here's the shipping page.

MARK   Thank you, Father.

GEORGE   We're having some tea before I go.

HELEN   Would you like some?

MARK   Yes, please.

HELEN   I'll get another cup.

              HELEN exits to the kitchen.

MARK   Dad, there's something—

GEORGE	Shh, listen carefully. There is going to be rioting in the streets. I have been ordered to lead the front line and to crush the demonstrators. The army forms the second line. Which means there will be shooting. If anything happens to me— You are the man of the house now—take care of your mother—

HELEN enters with a cup for MARK.

HELEN	Here we are.
GEORGE	Now, what's that you wanted to say?

MARK looks at his parents.

HELEN	You're looking a little pale, are you feeling alright?
MARK	Campbell....

GEORGE and HELEN look at MARK.

HELEN	Yes?

A moment.

MARK	Nothing.

HELEN pours tea for MARK, and then herself. Each person takes sugar and milk. GEORGE opens his newspaper and reads. MARK does the same with the shipping page. They sip their tea.

Sound of demonstrators chanting. Suddenly, an explosion. GEORGE, HELEN, and MARK look up. GEORGE looks out the window.

GEORGE	Lock the doors. Stay inside.

GEORGE exits. MARK grabs his binoculars and rushes to the window. Sound of the demonstrators comes closer and closer during the following scene.

HELEN	Mark, come away from the window.
MARK	Where are they? Where are they?
HELEN	Who?
MARK	I can't see them!

> MARK *puts the binoculars down and starts to exit.* HELEN *stops him. They struggle.*

HELEN	Where do you think you're going?
MARK	I have to find them. I have to find them.
HELEN	You can't go out.
MARK	I have to. I have to. Matthew and Campbell, they are in that mob.
HELEN	What?
MARK	There! Down there at the bottom of the hill. Matthew says he's going to bomb something, and Campbell's going to help.
HELEN	Oh, my God! *(grabs binoculars)* Where?
MARK	You can't see them. There's too many people. I'm going down to stop them.

> MARK *exits. Chanting becomes closer, louder.*

HELEN	Mark, no!

> *A cacophony: In the street, demonstrators shout. Helicopters overhead, jeeps arrive, sirens, patriotic communist music, etc.*
>
> *Lights up on* GEORGE, MATTHEW, *and* CAMPBELL *in three separate areas.*

Voice-over repeated throughout, getting louder and more insistent:

VOICE Unite! Unite! Unite!
Defeat imperial aggression.
Monsters will be destroyed.
No rest 'til victory is ours.
Down with U.S. imperialism.
Down with British imperialism.
Down with Soviet revisionists.
Long live the thoughts of Chairman Mao.
Long, long life to him.

MATTHEW C'mon, before they form ranks.

GEORGE *(using megaphone)* This demonstration is illegal!

CAMPBELL Hold your ground.

MATTHEW Six bombs to throw.

CAMPBELL No more compromise!

MATTHEW Who will come with me?

CAMPBELL No more sacrifice!

GEORGE Leave the area!

MATTHEW They are Running Dogs!

CAMPBELL Paper Tigers!

MATTHEW Six of the best!

GEORGE Disperse immediately!

CAMPBELL Your mother fucked foreigners and got a yellow bastard like you.

MATTHEW Total destruction.

CAMPBELL Running Dog, Paper Tiger.

MATTHEW	Running Dog, Paper Tiger.
	Lights up on HELEN *and* MARK *in separate areas.*
MARK	Matthew!
	CAMPBELL *and* MATTHEW *chant together:*
CAMPBELL	Running Dog, Paper Tiger, Running Dog, Paper Tiger.... *(repeat)*
MATTHEW	Running Dog, Paper Tiger, Running Dog, Paper Tiger.... *(repeat)*
GEORGE	This is your final warning. Disperse now!
HELEN	Sergeant, I'm looking for my boy.
CAMPBELL	You are traitors to your own people.
HELEN	Where?
MARK	Matthew!
HELEN	Please, sir, the Sergeant said I should talk to you.
GEORGE	Disperse in ten seconds! Ten... nine...
	GEORGE *counts down during the following, beating his shield with each count.*
HELEN	What do you mean?
MATTHEW	Bomb them now.
CAMPBELL	Wait.
MATTHEW	Shit!
HELEN	What do you mean, no!

MARK	I'm saying yes.
MATTHEW	Now!
CAMPBELL	Chant to build strength: Running Dog, Paper Tiger, Running Dog, Paper Tiger.... *(etc)*
HELEN	My children are in danger.
MATTHEW	Fuck the chant. I'm ready—
CAMPBELL	Chant, damn you.
MATTHEW	"There is a tide in the affairs of men...."
HELEN	I demand you let me through.
MARK	Let me through.

GEORGE *and* CAMPBELL *shout simultaneously:*

GEORGE	Wait for my signal.
CAMPBELL	Wait for my signal.

GEORGE *continues to count down:*

GEORGE	Two... ONE!

GEORGE *and* CAMPBELL *shout simultaneously:*

GEORGE	NOW!
CAMPBELL	NOW!
MARK	Stop! Stop!
HELEN	Oh, my God. Oh, my God.

> MARK *screams. Sudden silence.*
> GEORGE *clubs* MATTHEW, *who falls.*
> GEORGE *sees who he has hit and kneels*
> *beside the body.* CAMPBELL *clubs*
> GEORGE *three times.* GEORGE *falls.*
> *Blackout.*
>
> *A series of slides from the Hong Kong*
> *riots of 1967, showing crowds clashing*
> *with police, who are attacking*
> *demonstrators, their clubs swinging, faces*
> *contorted, bloodied heads, shoulders, legs,*
> *etc.*
>
> *Scene then returns to Hong Kong, 1987.*
> *Lights up on the chapel from the*
> *beginning of Act One.* MARK *and*
> MATTHEW *are silent for a while, then:*

MARK   Saunders Funeral Home, Causeway Bay....

CAMPBELL   Thank you.

> CAMPBELL *moves toward the door. He*
> *stops.*

You knew for twenty years, why didn't you tell me?

> *Pause.*

MARK   You left.

CAMPBELL   Not willingly.... When I struck him— I had often thought about it, wanted it, planned it in my mind's eye, but when it actually happened.... They pulled me away, and smuggled me into China.... Your father....

MARK   He died about six months after....

CAMPBELL   I'm sorry.... And Matthew?

MARK   He's alive.

CAMPBELL	Good, good.... I wouldn't have stayed away if I knew I had a mother and brothers.... But I didn't know, and so I found myself another family. I became a son of the Party.
MARK	Yes... a loyal son who was sent to the Sorbonne.... What do they call you now? "Special Advisor on Hong Kong Affairs"? You've done well.
CAMPBELL	And you. Scholarship to Cambridge. A seat on the Stock Exchange, a house on the Peak... and Sarah.
MARK	Your "family" wants to change all that.
CAMPBELL	Loyalty to the Party is expected. I can't betray their commitment to me.... I have learned to become who I am.... And you?

Pause. SARAH enters.

SARAH	Darling. Matthew is here, we should go to the funeral home.
CAMPBELL	Matthew.
MARK	Bring him in, please.

SARAH *exits.*

CAMPBELL	What will you do now?
MARK	I have three passports from three different countries.
CAMPBELL	Leave?
MARK	Yes.
CAMPBELL	I see....

SARAH *enters with* MATTHEW, *who is in a wheelchair.* CAMPBELL *turns and sees* MATTHEW.

MARK	Perhaps now you understand.

CAMPBELL *crouches to be at eye level with* MATTHEW.

CAMPBELL *(to* MATTHEW*)* I didn't know.

CAMPBELL *places his hand on* MATTHEW*'s.*

My old friend....

CAMPBELL *looks at* MARK.

(to MARK*)* Now that you have shown me... what are we fighting for?

MATTHEW *slowly holds his hand up, as though he were holding a sword.*

MATTHEW All for one.

Stillness. Curtain.

The End.